"As my sprint for justice has shifted to a marathon for justice, I have learned that soul care is not an indulgent luxury or a distraction. Rather, it is simultaneously the work of justice and the sustenance that fuels the work. In my soul's journey I have looked to April Yamasaki as a trusted guide. I read everything she writes! In the *Four Gifts*, her powerful insights are on brilliant display. With an integrative mind-body-spirit approach and the rich wisdom of a woman of color's life well spent, Yamasaki leads us on a journey that is worth following."

—**CHRISTENA CLEVELAND**, associate professor at Duke Divinity
School and author of *Disunity in Christ*

"April Yamasaki's *Four Gifts* was just what I needed just when I needed it. Her honest confessions felt like they were coming from a close friend who was teaching me how to rest in this hurried world, to find peace in the now, and to embrace God in each moment. Step aside. Open these pages. In your hurry, seek self-care and let the four gifts become your friends."

—**CHRIS MAXWELL**, pastor and author of *Pause with Jesus* and
Underwater

"*Four Gifts* is the most thorough and thoughtful exploration of self-care I have ever come across. With wisdom and sensitivity, April Yamasaki lays out the spiritual case for self-care and how to pursue it in harmony with life's other treasures, including vocation, community, and justice. This wonderful book will show you how proper self-care is not selfish but a healthy component of a mature, humble, and generous life."

—**DORCAS CHENG-TOZUN**, author of *Start, Love, Repeat*

"Amid the busyness of life, we look for ways to connect with God. *Four Gifts* creates the bridge to ease the journey. April Yamasaki's experience as a pastor and author forges a book that is eminently practical. *Four Gifts* enables conscious choices to simplify the journey, allowing for significant encounters with God."

—**SHARON R. HOOVER**, author o

"April Yamasaki lives what she writes about in *Four Gifts*. The book is full-of-Scripture inspirational, conversation-over-a-cup-of-tea personal, and down-to-earth practical. Any book on self-care that includes a chapter on lament as self-care has a unique contribution to make to the genre."

—**GARETH BRANDT**, author of *Under Construction*

"We all need to feed our souls, and April Yamasaki uses the two great commandments as a frame to help us do that. When we love God with all our heart, soul, mind, and strength, our growth becomes collateral benefit. No 'self-help' here, but spiritual nourishment."

—**CHARLES AARON**, associate professor at Perkins School of Theology

"I am touched by April Yamasaki's intimacy with Scripture, her perceptive self-understanding, and her keen ability to draw practical illustrations and suggestions for self-care from nearly every aspect of life. Many weary pastors, homemakers, and public servants will find abundant practical help through this book."

—**PALMER BECKER**, author of *Anabaptist Essentials*

"A delight to read. April Yamasaki blends scriptural insights with honest stories. She explores the tension of self-care and self-sacrifice, discipline and flexibility, self-awareness and self-indulgence. She gives practical suggestions for living a compassionate life that includes even ourselves. Reading this book is like having a deep conversation with a faithful friend."

—**CAROL PENNER**, assistant professor at Conrad Grebel University College

"*Four Gifts* is a virtual clinic for self-care. April Yamasaki opens the door and gently invites us in to a life of caring for our hearts, minds, bodies, and souls. She reminds us that this clinic is not a destination in itself but a place for renewal that enables us to continue to serve God and our neighbors. I found myself wanting to revisit this clinic often, both for the encouragement to take the time for self-care and for the valuable tools she has provided."

—**SHARLA FRITZ**, author of *Waiting* and *Soul Spa*

four gifts

four gifts

SEEKING SELF-CARE FOR HEART, SOUL, MIND, AND STRENGTH

APRIL YAMASAKI

HERALD
P R E S S
Harrisonburg, Virginia

Herald Press
PO Box 866, Harrisonburg, Virginia 22803
www.HeraldPress.com

Library of Congress Cataloging-in-Publication Data
Names: Yamasaki, April, author.
Title: Four gifts : seeking self-care for heart, soul, mind, and strength /
   April Yamasaki.
Description: Harrisonburg : Herald Press, 2018.
Identifiers: LCCN 2018014729| ISBN 9781513803340 (pbk. : alk. paper) |
   ISBN 9781513803357 (hardcover : alk. paper)
Subjects: LCSH: Spiritual life--Christianity. | Christian life.
Classification: LCC BV4501.3 .Y345 2018 | DDC 248.4--dc23 LC record
available at https://lccn.loc.gov/2018014729

FOUR GIFTS
© 2018 by April Yamasaki. Released by Herald Press, Harrisonburg, VA
22803. 800-245-7894. All rights reserved.
Library of Congress Control Number: 2018014729
International Standard Book Number: 978-1-5138-0334-0 (paperback);
978-1-5138-0335-7 (hardcover); 978-1-5138-0336-4 (ebook)
Printed in United States of America
Cover and interior design by Reuben Graham

22 21 20 19 18   10 9 8 7 6 5 4 3 2 1

For Gary,
who dreamed this book along with me
and heard every word first

Contents

Foreword

Several years ago a counselor suggested I do some self-care. After years of pushing to prove myself, to do and be more, and to live up to my own perfectionistic standards, this was something I sorely needed.

So my husband set up a deck chair, put a book in my hand, and sent me out the back door. I agreed to five minutes of relaxation and reading just for fun. At first it was so hard that I had to set a timer so I would stop watching the clock. But it only took five minutes for me to discover the appeal. When the timer went off, I set it for ten minutes more. A couple of times.

The exercise itself was valuable, but I probably learned even more from recognizing how challenging it was for me. I had become so disconnected from my own needs and natural rhythms that they didn't even register with me anymore. And I needed permission from myself to care for myself. I started intentionally incorporating self-care into my life. This has meant wrestling with questions about what makes my life matter; what it means to follow Christ; and what it means to honor God through rest.

I'm not alone in my challenge around self-care, nor in the lack of permission I gave myself. On any given day, the majority of North American workers are living with a high level of stress. Most workers don't take—or don't stop working on—the vacation days they earn. And when we do relax, most of us do so by watching television—a habit that can lower our stress levels but isn't the best way to care for overtaxed minds and bodies. Those who are not in the workforce—students, full-time parents, retirees, and others—often live highly demanding lives or may fill their days with activity while neglecting to care for themselves.

From my perspective as a leadership coach, it's quite obvious that many people believe caring for ourselves is selfish. That self-care equals self-indulgence. I talk with people who know what they need and withhold it from themselves, afraid to admit they might actually enjoy—or even desperately need—a night off. I also regularly talk with people who have no idea what they need.

Frankly, many of our churches thrive on this point of view. We are quick to reward those within our congregations who give of themselves until they have nothing left to give. Many congregations are running on the fumes of a few sacrificial people who exhaust themselves in misguided attempts to live as God would have them live.

This approach to life takes a heavy toll. The opposite of self-care is self-neglect. Neglect in any arena is a tragic failure to appreciate and nurture what God has lovingly created. Self-neglect means also failing to tend the object of God's great calling. Such indifference is hard to justify. And those who refuse to care for body, mind, spirit, and soul will eventually require rescue from the effects of their own demands.

Most of us simply never run out of things to do. That means we have to take intentional action to care for ourselves. And all these steps start with granting ourselves permission.

You're holding a helpful, permission-granting book. In *Four Gifts*, April Yamasaki will help you find full permission to care for yourself, rooted in the creative design and gracious invitation of our loving God.

If you're like me, you want to know how God sees your human needs and what God's Word says about self-care. You'll appreciate Yamasaki's sensible and biblically honest approach to the topic. She wrestles with the hard questions and acknowledges the ways in which caring for ourselves can seem antithetical to living for Christ. "To live this abundant, self-giving life of following Jesus, self-care must also make room somehow for self-surrender," she writes. "Can it be that we are called to both self-care and self-denial?"

I appreciate this book's wholistic view of self-care. We are complex beings, and both psychology and neurology have shown that our emotions, thoughts, and behaviors all influence each other. Foundational to all of them is what we believe. Belief and self-care are deeply connected, and as in other areas of life, our habits will reflect our beliefs. Self-care challenges our beliefs—especially those that reinforce our understanding of ourselves as self-sufficient and all-important to the proper functioning of life on planet Earth: "Surprise, surprise! Everyone—and everything—does not depend on me, and that includes my own self-care," writes Yamasaki. "Instead of the self-sufficiency of *self*-care, I can depend on the all-sufficiency of *God's* care."

Now there's a challenge. Our embrace of self-care is best rooted in our understanding of God's care, which does not waver or weaken with exercise. When we truly believe that both we and our world are lovingly supported and sustained by the God who made all that is, we understand that we are both more valuable than we suspected and less important than we thought.

I need these lessons on a regular basis, and I appreciate the gracious and inviting way Yamasaki presents them in *Four Gifts*. For today, I'm going to cherish this particular one: "I understand healthy self-care as 'me too' rather than 'me first' or 'me not at all.'" As I care for others and seek to live by the ways of the One who made me and put me here, I need to live with a "me too" in mind.

You too.

—**Amy Simpson,**
    author of *Blessed Are the Unsatisfied*,
    Anxious, and *Troubled Minds*

Introduction: Seeking Self-Care

Self-care is any action you purposefully take to improve your physical, emotional or spiritual well being.
—ELEANOR BROWNN

One Saturday morning, I wake to the sound of rain on my window and lie still for a moment, with my eyes closed. After a full week of too-busy days and nights on the go, this rare moment of solitude feels like a great gift. Instead of quickly getting up and on with my day as usual, and instead of reaching for my cell phone immediately like 46 percent of Americans say they do before getting up in the morning, I savor this precious time.[1] Instead of caring for

---

1. "For Most Smartphone Users, It's a 'Round-the-Clock' Connection," ReportLinker Insight, January 26, 2017, https://www.reportlinker.com/insight/smartphone-connection .html. According to the ReportLinker survey, 46 percent of Americans typically check their phones as soon as they wake up; 66 percent of eighteen- to twenty-four-year-olds do.

others, in this moment, I'm taking care of myself and resting in God's care.

For me, self-care has been a deep breath and sacred pause, a meandering walk along the waterfront, the *New York Times* crossword on a Sunday afternoon, a dish of stir-fried rice with greens and almonds after too many days of dairy products have made me feel tired and weighed down.

Self-care means taking all my vacation days even though 43 percent of my fellow working Canadians don't take all of theirs.[2] It means keeping an off-and-on journal, with page after page of random thoughts, poems, and prayers when the mood strikes—and page after page of blanks when it doesn't. Self-care as journaling and not-journaling means I'm free to write or doodle or ignore the empty page at any time.

Self-care makes my busy week possible. It allows me to survive and thrive in ministry today, and it has seen me through tough and tender times of caring for aging parents and undergoing my husband's diagnosis, surgery, and recovery from cancer, followed by the traumatic loss of his job. "Take good care of yourself," my friends urged me. Looking back, I realize now just how much I needed to do that. Self-care meant sanity, a hedge against being overwhelmed by circumstances beyond my control.

Yet if taking care of myself is so essential to daily living, why do I so often struggle with self-care? Why do I put it off, telling myself I'll do it tomorrow, or the next day, or the next? If I value it so much, why do I so frequently fail to practice it?

---

2. "Many Canadians Don't Take Allotted Vacation Time," Benefits Canada, March 24, 2014, www.benefitscanada.com/benefits/health-wellness/many-canadians-dont-take-allotted-vacation-time-50731.

MY STRUGGLE WITH SELF-CARE

For all the practical benefits of self-care, I don't always take the time for it. When I get busy, I neglect my morning work-out. I stay up too late, and get up too early. I eat the wrong things that taste good but make me feel bad. Sometimes self-care seems beyond my reach or forgotten altogether.

When a friend asked me recently about my next book, I replied rather sheepishly, "Well, it's supposed to be on self-care—ironic, I know, since I need to take better care of myself these days."

"That's often how it is with those in the helping professions," he said. As a social worker and counselor, he could identify with my dilemma. "We're not always good at taking our own advice."

Part of my struggle is simply being human. We don't always do what we know to be good and true for us. As the apostle Paul wrote long ago about his own inner conflict, "I do not understand my own actions" (Romans 7:15). The good that he wanted to do, he did not do. And the bad that he wanted to avoid, he ended up doing. That sounds a lot like me and self-care—not eating right even though I want to, and staying up too late even though I don't want to.

But my struggle with self-care runs even deeper.

ISN'T SELF-CARE SELFISH?

In a world in which many don't have enough to eat, do I really need to treat myself to all-you-can-eat sushi, even if it's only once in a while? Do I need that scoop of chocoholic ice cream, even if it's only one and I haven't had any dairy in days, and skip the cone please, I'll just have it in a dish? And why does my supposed self-care so often take the form of food anyway?

Throughout my childhood, most of my summer vacations were spent at home with long, lazy days of reading library books, playing badminton in the backyard, and roaming the neighborhood with my friends. Today we'd call that a "staycation," as if it's somehow unusual to stay at home instead of driving down the coast or flying to Hawaii, as if vacationing at home couldn't be a real vacation.

But what of those who live on the edge of just meeting their expenses, who can't afford to travel? Or those who have been displaced by famine, oppression, or violence, and who long for home—dreaming not of vacation, but of being able to stay in one place? For many in my community and around the world, there is no such thing as a vacation away from home or even a staycation at home. So why do I somehow need to get away in the name of good self-care?

"I avoided self-care because it looked dangerously close to self-indulgence," writes Amie Patrick, and I find myself nodding in agreement.[3] In light of human needs at home and around the world and all the many displaced and suffering people, in light of environmental concerns and the continuing strain on the planet, isn't my concern for self-care rather selfish?

THE LIMITS OF SELF-CARE

What's more, much of the popular self-care advice I read seems to add to my burden instead of lifting it, for now I must make time to go cloud watching, start a compliments diary, declutter

---

3. Amie Patrick, "Self-Care and Self-Denial," The Gospel Coalition, August 10, 2015, https://www.thegospelcoalition.org/article/self-care-and-self-denial.

my closets, or tack on some other self-care activity. Somehow, simplifying my life turns out to be more complicated than I'd hoped. Instead of relieving my already too-long to-do list, self-care becomes just one more thing to do.

On top of that, I sense the unspoken assumption—if not imposed by others, then perhaps of my own making—that if I could only practice better self-care, if I could ever finally do it right, then all would be well. I'd be happier and healthier. I'd finally be able to take care of everyone and everything.

But that's not the way life works. I'm human and limited, and you are too. There are only so many hours in a day, and only so much get-up-and-go before it's gone. Although we are human beings with considerable energy and creativity, we remain finite creatures with finite energies and finite time. We can't take care of everyone and everything on our own, no matter how much we practice self-care or how good we get at it.

The bigger picture is that we don't have to—for we have a God who cares for us. Instead of focusing narrowly on caring for myself, I can cast all my cares on God, who cares for me and who cares for all of us. As 1 Peter 5:10 reminds us, God longs to "restore, support, strengthen, and establish" us. Surprise, surprise! Everyone—and everything—does not depend on me, and that includes my own self-care. Instead of the self-sufficiency of *self*-care, I can depend on the all-sufficiency of *God's* care.

At the same time, I find myself challenged by the teaching and example of Jesus, for in the course of his public ministry, Jesus issued a clear call to commitment and self-denial.

JESUS AND THE OPPOSITE OF SELF-CARE

"If any want to become my followers, let them deny themselves and take up their cross and follow me," said Jesus. "For
those who want to save their life will lose it, and those who
lose their life for my sake, and for the sake of gospel, will save
it" (Mark 8:34-35).

Isn't that the opposite of self-care? If Jesus cared about self-
care, would he have allowed himself to be arrested, brutalized,
and put to death on a cross? If Jesus' first followers thought
about self-care, would those men and women have left their
homes and livelihoods to follow him around the countryside?
Would the apostle Paul have suffered flogging, stoning, shipwreck, and other hardships, only to keep on preaching and
suffering for the sake of the gospel?

Instead of caring for themselves, those who followed Jesus
denied themselves and found a new way of life in God's kingdom. They served with such wholehearted abandon that I
suspect our twenty-first-century North American concern for
self-care would have made no sense to them. They put into
practice these words that I've often sung, yet can never quite
live out:

> All to Jesus I surrender,
> all to Him I freely give;
> I will ever love and trust Him,
> in His presence daily live.
> I surrender all, I surrender all;
> all to Thee, my blessed Savior,
> I surrender all.[4]

---

4. Judson W. Van DeVenter, "All to Jesus I Surrender" (1896).

For as much as I need self-care, I also hear this call to self-surrender. I, too, long to serve with such self-forgetfulness, abandon, and trust: to spend time with a family as they mourn the loss of their loved one, to lose myself in a piece of writing and suddenly realize hours later that I've forgotten to eat my breakfast. Such times of self-surrender offer deep joy and, I believe, a taste of God's kingdom.

To live this abundant, self-giving life of following Jesus, self-care must also make room somehow for self-surrender. Can it be that we are called to both self-care and self-denial? Is that a healthy tension, a living paradox—or is it simply impossible? As Jonathan Clauson, producer of the Christ and Pop Culture *Persuasion* podcast, notes, "Finding a balance between tending to your self and soul . . . and pouring out your life for the benefit of others is a tricky one."[5]

FOUR GIFTS

For all these reasons, I find myself still seeking self-care: because I know I need self-care yet can't always get there; because I'm tired of seeing self-care as just one more thing to do; and because I need a bigger vision of caring for myself that also embraces caring for others and surrendering myself to God's call and care.

As part of my search, this book explores four gifts drawn from the words of Jesus to "love the Lord your God with all your *heart*, and with all your *soul*, and with all your *mind*, and with all your *strength*" and to "love your neighbor as yourself" (Mark 12:30-31, emphasis added). These four gifts offer

5. Jonathan Clauson, "Persuasion: Living the Hygge Life," Christ and Pop Culture, February 7, 2017, https://christandpopculture.com/living-the-hygge-life-persuasion-podcast.

a framework of self-care that includes (1) our total well-being, represented by the heart; (2) our spiritual well-being, represented by the soul; (3) our mental well-being, represented by the mind; (4) our physical well-being, represented by strength.

Along the way, I'll address specific self-care challenges like setting priorities, self-care in a digital world, and getting a good night's sleep. I'll share some personal stories, biblical and theological insights, and suggestions for self-care—not as more items for your to-do list but as gifts to play with, pray over, or simply set aside for some other time. I've also included reflection questions in many of the sections that may be used for journaling or discussion with a group. Please join me, and we can explore these four gifts of self-care together.

Part I

HEART

1

The Heart of Self-Care

Taking care of yourself doesn't mean me first; it means me too.
—L. R. KNOST

One summer I celebrated worship and communion outdoors with several thousand other hearty souls. We gathered in a huge field to sing our praises to God, and every tenth person or so had been given a brown paper bag with bread and juice to share. Our picnic blankets, spread out on the grass, became tables of communion as we ate and drank together.

As a final blessing, our worship leaders invited everyone to participate in an interactive call-and-response. They would say a line, and we were to respond each time with either "Oh yes he did!" or "Oh no he didn't!" We had no printed liturgy, no words on a screen—just our ears to listen and our voices to answer back.

"Jesus said, 'The kingdom of God is among you,'" said one of our worship leaders, and we all responded, "Oh yes he did!"

"Jesus said, 'I send you out as sheep among wolves. Be as wise as serpents and as gentle as doves.'" Again we all responded, "Oh yes he did!"

"Jesus said, 'Love your neighbor and your enemy and yourself.'" All around me, people were calling out, "Oh yes he did!" I seemed to be the only spoilsport adding at the end, "Oh no he didn't!"

Because Jesus never actually said, "Love yourself."

Or did he?

IS THERE A THIRD GREAT COMMANDMENT?

In his Sermon on the Mount, Jesus said to his closest followers, "Love your enemies and pray for those who persecute you" (Matthew 5:44). Then, later, when a scribe asked him for the greatest commandment, Jesus replied with the double commandment to love God and neighbor: "The first is, 'Hear, O Israel: the Lord our God, the Lord is one; you shall love the Lord your God with all your heart, and with all your soul, and with all your mind, and with all your strength.' The second is this, 'You shall love your neighbor as yourself.' There is no other commandment greater than these" (Mark 12:29-31).

Jesus certainly demonstrated his love for God; he regularly spent time in worship and prayer and understood his entire life and ministry to be grounded in God's Word. As he healed the sick, cast out demons, forgave sins, and preached good news to the poor, he showed love for his neighbors—and that included the people of his own Jewish community as well as those considered marginalized, outcast, and enemy. Just as he taught his followers, Jesus prayed for those who persecuted him. For those who arrested, tortured, and executed him, he prayed, "Father, forgive them; for they do not know what they are doing" (Luke 23:34).

Clearly, in his teaching and by the way he lived, Jesus said to love your neighbor and your enemy—oh yes, he did! But the closest he came to telling us to love ourselves appears only as an aside: You shall love your neighbor "as yourself." His side comment might assume that we already love ourselves, but Jesus doesn't present this as a command equal to his instruction and example to love others. In his discussion with the scribe and in the rest of his life and teaching, Jesus' emphasis falls squarely on loving God and loving neighbor.

New Testament scholar Timothy Geddert makes this point:

> Some have suggested that there is an implied third great commandment, to love . . . yourself ([Mark] 12:31). This, however, misses the point of the passage. The text refers to an active, caring love that invests heart, soul, mind, and strength in the service of God and others. To love others adequately requires a redirection of these energies. Instead of active investment of our energies to serve ourselves, we are called to active investment of them in the service of God and others (cf. 10:43-45). While a healthy self-esteem is compatible with (and perhaps necessary for) a self-giving love of God and others, that is not what this text is teaching.[1]

So did Jesus say to love yourself? Oh no, he didn't. Or not exactly. If there were a third great commandment about loving

---

1. Timothy J. Geddert, *Mark*, Believers Church Bible Commentary (Scottdale, PA: Herald Press, 2001), 290.

yourself, Jesus certainly didn't state it as plainly as he did the other two.

The sixteenth-century reformer John Calvin wrote that loving God and others must come first, for "we are too much devoted to ourselves."[2] However, early church fathers like Tertullian, Chrysostom, and Augustine read this same text as giving priority to self-love.[3] If we do not love ourselves first, how are we to love our neighbor *as* ourselves?

While some might wish for a single consistent understanding of these words of Jesus, I appreciate the healthy tension between these two views. For when I am overly stern with myself and forever putting myself in last place, the early church fathers remind me to love myself and so love God and neighbor. And when I am too much devoted to myself and becoming self-centered, the reformer reminds me of the priority to love God and neighbor. In navigating between these two poles, I find the place of authentic and wholesome self-care.

Which of these two readings of the text do you most need at this point in your life? Can you also see value in the alternate reading to provide a healthy balance?

WHO'S ON FIRST

In contrast to Jesus' emphasis on loving God and neighbor, the concern for self-care often puts loving ourselves in first

2. John Calvin, *Commentary on Matthew, Mark, Luke*, vol. 3, CCEL Edition v1.0 (Grand Rapids, MI: Christian Classics Ethereal Library, 1999), 39, http://www.ccel.org/ccel/calvin/calcom33.html.
3. Lamar Williamson Jr., *Mark*, Interpretation: A Bible Commentary for Teaching and Preaching (Louisville, KY: John Knox Press, 1983), 228.

place. After all, as the logic goes, if you don't love yourself, you can't love anyone else. If you don't take care of yourself first, you can't take care of anyone else. It's like the airplane safety talk: if the oxygen masks come down, put on your own mask first before helping your child or anyone else. That's good practical sense. That's good self-care that enables us to care for others.

Jesus certainly took time for what we might call self-care today. After an intense forty-day struggle with Satan, he took time to rest in God's care before beginning his public ministry. After a day of healings that stretched long into evening, he made sure he had time alone the next day even though people were searching for him. When his disciples became so busy that they hardly had time to eat, he urged them to get away to rest.

Yet just as often, Jesus set aside his own self-care so that he could serve God and show compassion to others. When he heard that Herod had John the Baptist beheaded while in prison, Jesus went to a secluded place alone. But when the crowds followed him, he set aside his personal mourning and spent his time healing those who were sick. When evening came, instead of sending the crowds away, he again set aside his own self-care and fed them. Only then did he dismiss the crowds, send his disciples ahead by boat, and finally find time alone to grieve John's death.

On the night of his arrest, Jesus knew full well that he would be tortured and crucified. He had spoken to his disciples on three separate occasions of his coming suffering and death. That night he prayed for release even as he prayed for God's will to be done. Yet instead of retreating to the relative safety and obscurity of the countryside, instead of defending himself, he sacrificed his own needs and went to the cross. As Jesus had said to his disciples earlier in his ministry, "My food is to do the will of him who sent me and to complete his work" (John 4:34).

To the extent that Jesus practiced self-care, I can't say that he practiced self-care by putting himself first. While he clearly valued rest for himself and others, he would also at times deliberately choose to set aside his own need for rest. He set aside his own life in order to complete the task that God had set before him. Instead of "me first," Jesus' life was radically shaped by his two core commitments to love God and neighbor.

Of course, I'm not Jesus. But in my search for self-care, both his teaching and example ring true for me. When there's a death in my congregation, I don't refuse to spend time with a grieving family because I need to take care of myself. Young parents often set aside their own need for sleep to tend to one of their children in the middle of the night, and not just once but night after night after night. Firefighters and other emergency personnel regularly risk their own safety for the sake of others. Yes, we all need self-care. But self-care doesn't always come first, and it's shaped by our core commitments.

_____

In an emergency situation, putting on your own oxygen mask first allows you to breathe and think clearly enough to help someone else. What other situations might call for self-care first? In addition to the examples in the previous paragraph, what other situations might call for setting aside self-care for the sake of others?

_____

WHAT'S ON SECOND

In Scripture, the heart represents the center of our physical, mental, and spiritual being. It includes our thinking, our feelings, our will, our entire consciousness. The heart is a gift that directs our whole being and holds everything together. Our core commitments are like the heart, which directs everything else we do in a particular day and which even shapes our self-care.

As newlyweds, my husband and I were both university students, juggling his schedule and my schedule. Our days and nights included studying for classes and working part time, seeing friends and family, being involved in our church, and feeling pulled in many different directions. But every Friday night we set aside as "date night." We didn't use the language of self-care at the time, but that's really what it was: a time to set aside the push and pull of daily life and enjoy that time together.

We also didn't use the language of core commitments, but as I look back now, I can see how committed we were to our marriage and our studies, and how those core commitments shaped our self-care. Our self-care in the form of date night didn't exactly come first. For us, Friday was the end of our week, not the beginning. And if one of us had a big exam on Wednesday, then on Wednesday that exam came first. Yet self-care remained a key practice alongside our core commitments to each other and to our education.

Instead of "me first," self-care is really "me too." When parents set aside their own need for sleep to care for a sick child in the middle of the night, in that moment the child's need comes first. For the parent, self-care might be an afternoon nap when the child finally settles down, or time for a walk the next day. In this way, self-care that honors core commitments might be delayed or postponed or after the fact, but it's still self-care even if it sometimes seems to come in second.

For some, however, self-care is so far down the list that it never happens. Instead of self-care as "me too," it's self-neglect as "me not at all," which can lead to serious consequences.

In Japan, *karoshi* literally means "death by overwork," often due to suicide, heart attack, stroke, or other illness. When a journalist died at the age of thirty-one from heart failure, authorities classified her death as *karoshi* because of her extremely demanding job and work schedule. For years, she had taken little time off, logging as many as 159 hours of overtime in a single month. When a thirty-four-year-old maintenance worker died by suicide, his death was also deemed *karoshi*, again because of prolonged and massive overtime hours on the job. In 2015 in Japan, 189 deaths were officially attributed to *karoshi*, and others may well have gone unreported.[4]

The deaths of these workers at such young ages may well have been complicated by physical and mental health issues, medication side effects, social expectations, family and cultural dynamics, and other factors. Attributing *karoshi* solely to a lack of self-care would be too simplistic. Yet self-care was clearly lacking in the absence of healthy boundaries and a healthy rhythm of work and rest.

---

4. Eli Rosenberg, "Another Victim of the 'Karoshi' Curse," *Vancouver (B.C.) Sun*, October 7, 2017, NP5.

When have you set aside or postponed your own need for self-care? Was it a deliberate decision to postpone temporarily, for good reason, or was it an instance of neglect? How would you respond to the same situation now?

THE GIFT OF SELF-CARE: HONOR YOUR CORE COMMITMENTS

Given this larger landscape of self-care, and given the core commitments that shape our lives, I understand healthy self-care as "me too" rather than "me first" or "me not at all." So to begin, I find it most helpful to consider several questions: What are my core commitments, and how might they shape my self-care? How do I practice self-care—not always first, but in a way that is life-giving and sustaining for me and also allows me to honor my core commitments? Using the framework of Jesus' great commandment, how do I love God, love my neighbor, and still take care of myself?

The answers may well be different at different points in our lives. As a student and newlywed, I led a different life than I do today as a pastor and writer. The young mom, the father of teenagers, the business owner, the retiree, the person living with chronic pain, the activist: the whoever-you-are-today may have different core commitments and different self-care needs than the whoever-you-will-be-tomorrow. As a former educator and administrator said to me recently, "The solutions to life's problems keep changing, because our lives keep changing."

To reflect on your changing need for self-care, consider one or more of the following. Receive them as gifts to try or to skip as you choose. In other words, don't stress out over them. Use what you find helpful for now, and come back for more whenever you wish.

- **PRAYERFULLY REFLECT** on your core commitments. Are you caring for young children, aging parents, a spouse with health problems, or other significant relationships? Are vocational commitments or personal health issues at the core for you? As alternative ways of identifying your core commitments, think of your life purpose, your personal mission statement if you have one, what you would like to be known for, or the legacy you would like to leave behind.

- **IN WHAT WAYS** do your core commitments give opportunity for self-care? What challenges do they present?

- **TAKE A PERSONAL INVENTORY** of the self-care practices that already form part of your life. Which ones would you like to do more? Which ones may not be as life-giving as they once were?

- **CHOOSE ONE SELF-CARE PRACTICE** from your list and then follow through with it. Add it as a reminder on your phone or in your datebook. Or jot it down on a sticky note and post in a prominent place. Take time to take good care of yourself.

- **TURN TO THE CONTENTS PAGE** of this book and consider the four gifts: (1) our overall well-being, represented by the heart, (2) our spiritual well-being, represented by the soul; (3) our mental well-being, represented by the mind; (4) our physical well-being, represented by strength. Which of these is your strongest area of self-care? Which could use more attention?

2

Boundaries of the Heart

"No" is a complete sentence.
—ANNE LAMOTT

At the start of a workshop I lead on spiritual practice for busy people, I ask, "So what has made us such busy people this last week?" The question functions as an easy ice-breaker as I ask people to call out their answers. I write them on the flip chart. Work. Family. School. Church. Social media. Driving. Sports. Expectations and trying to meet them.

When the page is full, I turn to the next, and the next, and I keep writing. The answers get more specific as we warm up to the exercise, and I hear more murmurs of recognition—yes, we are busy people!

"For busy people, spiritual practice begins quite simply with stopping." I draw a vertical line through the busyness recorded on each page. "All these things might be good things that we want and need to do. But one way to begin attending to our spiritual life is learning how to stop. That might mean stopping our work at the end of a day or the end of a week. Or pausing to catch a breath between one meeting and the next. Or spending a quiet moment alone before the day begins. For anyone—and especially for busy people—spiritual practice begins with stopping."

When it comes to self-care, stopping is also a good place to begin. Quite literally, self-care starts when we stop.

I used to think that self-care meant *adding* something, especially something fun and self-pampering. Like going out to dinner in the middle of the week. Or an hour of retail therapy on a Saturday afternoon. Or getting a massage, just because. Or making time for all three. I'm all for some fun as part of healthy self-care, but rather than adding on more things, what if self-care begins with learning how to stop?

PUTTING ON THE BRAKES

In *Boundaries: When to Say Yes, How to Say No to Take Control of Your Life*, authors Henry Cloud and John Townsend tackle three key questions as outlined on the back cover:

Is your life out of control?

Do people take advantage of you?

Do you have trouble saying no?

The book begins with "A Day in a Boundaryless Life" and ends with "A Day in a Life with Boundaries," following Sherrie as she interacts with her husband, children, friend, coworker, mother, and others throughout her day. As Sherrie works at developing healthy personal boundaries, she becomes less frazzled and finds more satisfaction in her family, church, and work relationships, and those around her seem healthier, too, as they adjust to her newfound life with boundaries. The authors conclude their book with this note to their readers: "It's our prayer that your biblical boundaries will lead you to a life of love, freedom, responsibility, and service."[1]

I wish I had read this book early in my ministry when I needed to establish some healthy boundaries. Instead, I was so excited to be called as a pastor, and so eager to learn, that I said yes to every new opportunity. Serve on a denominational committee? Yes, I'd love to get to know the wider church and contribute where I can. Be a guest speaker at the local Bible college? Yes, I'd be glad to connect with students. Write a series of devotionals? Yes, I'd like to continue with my writing. Lead a weekend women's retreat? Yes, I'd be happy to prepare a few sessions and enjoy the time together. Yes. Yes. Yes.

But soon all those yeses piled up until I knew I had a big pile of trouble. They were all good opportunities—great opportunities, in fact, but just too many of them. My life had become too busy and overcrowded, with so many things competing for attention that I couldn't do justice to any of them. My life was out of control. I needed to start saying no. I needed boundaries. I needed self-care—not by adding something new to my life, but by learning how to stop.

---

1. Henry Cloud and John Townsend, *Boundaries: When to Say Yes, When to Say No to Take Control of Your Life* (Zondervan Publishing House, 1992), 296. The book is still in print with a slightly changed title, with over two million copies sold; related books like *Boundaries in Dating* and *Boundaries in Marriage Workbook* are also available.

How would you answer the questions posed by Henry Cloud and John Townsend: Is your life out of control? Do people take advantage of you? Do you have trouble saying no?

GOOD BOUNDARIES MAKE GOOD SELF-CARE

Along with our core commitments, healthy personal boundaries can help us determine when to say yes and when to say no—not just to "take control" of our lives, as the *Boundaries* subtitle suggests, but for healthy and abundant living as the authors describe throughout their book. Healthy boundaries keep us honest about our human and personal limitations. They remind us that we're not actually responsible for everything in the world or even in our own lives, so we don't need to act as if we are. In that way, healthy boundaries are essential for good self-care.

In my case, not only had I said yes to some invitations when I should have said no; I had actually volunteered for things that I later regretted. Some of this could be chalked up to my natural enthusiasm for new ministry and my keen desire to learn and to contribute, which were all good. But sometimes I had said yes because I didn't want to disappoint the person asking, or because I felt guilty saying no, or out of a misplaced sense of responsibility.

Good boundaries are essential for good self-care, not only for those in pastoral ministry but for all of us as part of daily living. For the student stressed out by a full course load plus two jobs and who always seems to get stuck with cleaning up after her housemates. For the employee who repeatedly covers for a colleague and works overtime to pick up the slack. For the senior tired of the friend who constantly asks to borrow money. Self-care in the form of a weekend away or some other treat can't address what these people really need. They need— we all need—self-care in the form of learning to say no, of establishing and maintaining healthy boundaries.

Jesus welcomed and reached out to a wide range of people. Rich men who were part of the establishment, like Nicodemus. Men of distasteful reputation, like Zacchaeus. Women who became close friends and followers, like Mary and Martha. Unnamed prostitutes, religious people, tax collectors, fisher-folk, a Roman centurion, people considered unclean, people in need of forgiveness and healing, men, women, and children.

Alongside this wide embrace, Jesus also lived and preached healthy boundaries. In the wilderness, he repeatedly turned down temptation, turning away from Satan to affirm his faith in God again and again. His core commitment to serve God set a boundary for the way he lived. "Worship the Lord your God, and serve only him," he insisted. "Repent, and believe in the good news," he preached to the crowds. "You cannot serve God and wealth," he said to his followers (see Matthew 4:10; Mark 1:15; Matthew 6:24).

Letters to the early church set a clear boundary between acting spitefully and being kind to one another, and between living apart from God and living in Christ (see Ephesians 4:31-32; Romans 6:5-11). The letters underscored a clear boundary between being weighed down and being focused on following Jesus: "Therefore, since we are surrounded by so great a cloud of witnesses, let us also lay aside every weight and the sin that clings so closely, and let us run with perseverance the race that is set before us, looking to Jesus the pioneer and perfecter of our faith" (Hebrews 12:1-2).

The things I had taken on only to avoid disappointing others represented that excess "weight," which kept me from joyfully running with the other tasks and responsibilities that God had placed before me. Instead of respecting the boundary between what God had given me to carry and what was additional baggage belonging to someone else, I had taken on too much. It was past time to remove the extra weight and simplify my life.

As I worked at clearing my overloaded schedule, I learned some important lessons. First, I didn't need to worry about disappointing anyone, for people quickly moved on to someone else. And second, laying aside those things became an important element of self-care, not by adding a self-care practice but by removing those things that weren't mine to carry.

Have you ever said yes to something and then later wished you had said no? Or volunteered for something and then later wished you hadn't? Consider why you said yes or volunteered in the first place. And why did you then wish you hadn't? What can you learn from your experience?

BOUNDARIES OR BARRIERS

Over time I also learned that establishing good boundaries means much more than simply removing the pieces that don't fit—more than drawing a line in the sand and refusing to cross it. For while boundaries can help bring clarity and focus, when taken to the extreme and rigidly applied, boundaries can become barriers to compassion and living a full life. I think that's what happened with the priest and the Levite who refused to help the injured man they encountered on the road between Jerusalem and Jericho. Whatever commitments they may have had, whatever religious laws they were bound to keep—instead of healthy boundaries, these became unhealthy barriers to helping a fellow traveler in distress and dire need.

While Jesus had clear boundaries, he also knew when to make exceptions so that they did not become barriers. When he was on his way to heal Jairus's daughter, for example, Jesus stopped to proclaim healing on a woman who had reached out to him in desperation. He allowed himself to be interrupted even though he had a literal life-and-death commitment, even though Jairus was a leader of the synagogue and hurrying Jesus along to save his daughter.

When a Canaanite woman begged Jesus for help, he at first replied that he had come only to "the lost sheep of the house of Israel"—an apparent boundary that focused his ministry on the Jewish community. Yet when the woman persisted, Jesus did not treat this boundary as an absolute barrier. Instead, just as he had earlier healed the servant of a Roman centurion, he again responded with compassion for someone beyond the house of Israel. Jesus commended the Canaanite woman for her faith and healed her daughter (Matthew 15:21-28).

So how do we know when to abide by our personal boundaries and when to step over them? When does a healthy boundary become an unhealthy barrier? How do we even determine where our boundary lines fall? In the gospel accounts of Jesus' ministry,

I see that he mainly kept to "the lost sheep of the house of Israel" as he said, yet would move beyond his own community in response to the urgent need of those who came to him. In his response to the Canaanite woman, the woman's persistence and the dialogue between them also seemed to play a critical role.

What's more, in all his life and ministry, Jesus sought the will of God through prayer. He spent an extended time in fasting and prayer before announcing his public ministry. He prayed about the direction and scope of his work before, during, and after many miracles of compassion and healing. Even as Jesus prepared to give up his own life in crossing the biggest personal boundary of all, he prayed: "Father, if you are willing, remove this cup from me; yet, not my will but yours be done" (Luke 22:42).

The decisions we face in life may be far less weighty, yet the example of Jesus can instruct and guide us. He considered specific circumstances of urgency, he thoughtfully engaged in dialogue with others, and he prayerfully sought God's will for his life. These practices can form part of our practice today as well. Together they point the way to establishing healthy boundaries that allow us to take care of ourselves while also responding to others with compassion.

Some people may tend to say yes too quickly, to ignore their own boundaries even in the absence of any urgency or good reason. Others may tend to say no too quickly, to keep their boundaries rigid with little flexibility or compassion. Which tendency do you see within yourself, and how does that relate to your need for self-care?

THE GIFT OF SELF-CARE: CREATE AN I-DON'T-DO LIST

One self-care tool that helps me pay attention to healthy boundaries is my I-don't-do list. Some of the things on my list are practical time-savers. I don't do telephone surveys. I don't do personality tests that keep showing up in my Facebook feed. Others relate more directly to my physical and mental health. I don't drink caffeine every day, because I feel better without it. I don't try to please everyone, which would be impossible anyway. I don't beat myself up for not doing everything on my daily to-do list.

Of course, there are exceptions. When I travel across time zones, I find that coffee helps me adjust, so I might drink it more when I'm away. And sometimes I realize I'm twisting myself into a pretzel trying to please everyone, and I have to tell myself, "Wait a minute. That's on my I-don't-do list." The point is not to have a list of barriers and follow it robot-like to the letter of the law. Instead, the point is to outline some healthy self-care boundaries.

To create your own I-don't-do list, consider some of the following. Or if you already have a list, you may wish to revise it as necessary.

- **WHERE DO YOU NEED** to establish and maintain healthy boundaries? What do you need to stop doing so you can take care of yourself and devote more time and energy to your core commitments?

- **I STARTED WITH AN INFORMAL LIST** in my head, and only later began to record my I-don't-dos in my journal. But research suggests that students remember and learn more when they take notes by hand, so you may find it more helpful to start with a handwritten list.[2] Begin with the things that come to mind most immediately, and don't ignore those things that seem the most obvious. I've always known that it's impossible to please everyone, but adding it to my list has helped curb my tendency to try. Nothing is too obvious or too small for an I-don't-do list.

- **PAY ATTENTION** to practical time-savers, personal habits, and attitudes. One woman says she doesn't do gyms, but goes for long walks instead. Another doesn't watch television. One man refuses to own a cell phone. A mother of school-aged children gave up nagging for Lent, and it worked so well for both her and her family that it's now a permanent part of her I-don't-do list.

- **MAKE YOUR LIST** personal and realistic by including things that you already don't do. Realize that you've been developing healthy boundaries even if you've never thought of them that way.

- **MAKE YOUR LIST** aspirational: include things that you need to stop doing. It takes time to learn new patterns of behavior, but an I-don't-do list can help set direction.

- **COMMIT** your I-don't-do list to God in prayer. Think of it as a work in progress that changes and develops over time. Be kind to yourself as you seek to live it out.

---

2. Pam A. Mueller and Daniel M. Oppenheimer, "The Pen Is Mightier Than the Keyboard: Advantages of Longhand Over Laptop Note Taking," *Psychological Science* 25, no. 6 (June 2014): 1159–68.

3

Hearts in Community

For the task is too heavy for you; you cannot do it alone.
—EXODUS 18:18

When God first called Moses to lead the people out of Egypt, Moses responded with fear. "What shall I say?" he asked. "Suppose they do not believe me or listen to me. . . . I have never been eloquent, neither in the past nor even now" (Exodus 3:13; 4:1, 10). Yet God had called Moses, and by the gifting and power of God, Moses led the people out of Egypt and became a great leader. Not only did the people listen to him, but over time they came to rely on him even more than Moses could handle.

As the Hebrews continued on their way to the Promised Land, Moses continued to speak to God on behalf of the people. He directed their path into the wilderness and through the Red Sea. He led them in song and celebration upon their deliverance. When the people ran out of bread and water, they turned to Moses to solve their problems, and he did. He became the judge of any and all disputes.

Day after day, the people came to Moses so that he could instruct them in God's commands and settle any disagreements. So many people came to him that they would stand in line from morning to night, waiting to present their case and to hear his judgment. For all his earlier fears, Moses appeared to be a successful leader. But when his father-in-law, Jethro, saw this, he said to Moses, "What you are doing is not good. You will surely wear yourself out, both you and these people with you. For the task is too heavy for you; you cannot do it alone" (Exodus 18:17-18).

Instead, Jethro advised Moses to choose leaders, to instruct them in God's ways so they could serve as judges and refer only the most major cases to Moses. He said, "If you do this, and God so commands you, then you will be able to endure, and all these people will go to their home in peace" (Exodus 18:23).

Jethro's wise advice proved to be good *self*-care for Moses and good *community* care for the people. Appointing additional judges relieved Moses' burden of hearing cases day after day and left him with more energy for his key leadership role of representing the people before God. The new judges grew in knowledge, experience, and wisdom, empowered to contribute to community life in a new way with a new level of responsibility. And the community as a whole became less dependent on one person, with a new and healthier interdependence as they sought to follow God together.

I CAN'T DO IT ALL, AND YOU CAN'T EITHER

Instead of bristling at his father-in-law's advice, or dismissing it as unwanted meddling, Moses demonstrated an openness to listening to Jethro and to accepting his good counsel. Then he asked for help from those in the community willing to learn God's statutes and who could be trusted to serve the people ably and well. As Jethro had pointed out, Moses couldn't do everything himself, and he didn't have to. He could take care of himself and his community by engaging and enlisting the help of others.

Like Moses, I can't do everything by myself, and you can't either.

At times that might seem obvious. When I was sent home from the hospital after some surgery, I was told to get lots of rest and not lift anything heavy. No problem, since the general anesthetic had yet to wear off and I could barely get myself out of a chair. I wasn't about to start lifting weights. My husband drove me home. He made me tea and soup while I rested on the couch and did a crossword puzzle. When I dropped my pen, he picked it up so I wouldn't have to do it myself. My family called and sent cards. Church members and friends brought food, flowers, and stopped by to say hello. I didn't have to take care of myself alone, and my husband didn't have to care for me by himself either. We had lots of help.

When we're well, our need for help might not seem so obvious. Now I can lift weights in my morning workout, put in a full day at the church, make rice with curry chicken and cauliflower from scratch for supper, lead an evening meeting, come home to clean up the kitchen, and write my blog article for the next day. My writing friend with school-aged children does all that and more, except she gets up at four in the morning to write and works in an office.

Being on the go and multitasking every step of the way has become a way of life for many of us. In the busy blur of it all, we might even manage to snap a photo for our Instagram and add a clever hashtag to share. Yet in the back of my mind, I hear the voice of Jethro: "What you are doing is not good. You will surely wear yourself out, both you and these people with you. For the task is too heavy for you; you cannot do it alone."

As Moses discovered, I'm better off when I don't try to do everything myself. Instead of pushing myself until I'm running on empty, I can set some boundaries and invest my time and energy in my core commitments and other priorities. I can also let other people help me, which makes for better self-care and makes the people around me happier and healthier too.

Without Jethro's astute observation, Moses may not have realized how overloaded he had become. Have you ever taken on too much without realizing it? Who or what helped you to notice?

FROM ME TO WE

Whenever we invite someone over for dinner, they inevitably ask, "Can I bring something?" I love to cook, and I would gladly plan and make the whole meal myself. But whenever anyone asks, I always say yes. That means one less dish I need to prepare in our tiny kitchen, and more time for other things, which contributes to my self-care. At the same time, I can admire our guest's home-baked bread or garden-fresh salad or butter tarts from a local bakery, and we can all appreciate the creativity and generosity of their offering. By contributing together to the meal, we can each share our gifts and build healthy community.

Even Jesus did not do everything himself. He drew on his deep relationship with his Father. He relied on some of the women for financial support. He gathered together a community of disciples, to teach them and to send them out in service. When Jesus fed the crowds, a young boy offered his bread and fish, Andrew brought the boy to Jesus, and when Jesus had given thanks, the disciples distributed the food to the people.

The apostle Paul also worked with a ministry team of friends and followers of Jesus. At various times, he traveled with Silas, Barnabas, Timothy, and other companions. On his church planting mission through Philippi, he relied on the hospitality of a businesswoman named Lydia both before and after his imprisonment for preaching the gospel. The last chapter of his letter to the Romans offers a litany of coworkers, including Phoebe, Prisca and Aquila, Epaenetus, Mary, Andronicus and Junia, and many more.

When has your self-care meant receiving help from someone else? How did your relationship grow and change as a result?

WHEN SYSTEMS NEED CHANGING

Moses needed other people to help him. He had been so caught up in his daily routine that he didn't realize how unhealthy it had become. He needed Jethro's sharp observation and counsel. He needed other leaders to share the task of serving the people. At the same time, the community needed to grow into a new way of relating to him and to one another. The ancient story beautifully highlights how self-care and community care work together.

Moses might have received some temporary relief by taking breaks throughout his day and by setting aside his work on the Sabbath. Eating and sleeping well and going for long walks might have helped to sustain his energy. But the one-man system of justice was inherently unstable and unhealthy, and no amount of personal self-care could make it right. The system itself had to change.

The early church faced a similar challenge. Rapid growth in numbers meant rapid growth in ministry to meet the needs of the people. Those who owned property sold their land and buildings, then donated the proceeds to be redistributed to those in need. Widows received special attention with a daily distribution of food. In a world without social assistance from government or other agencies, in the absence of food stamps and food banks, such sharing became a distinctive mark of Christian community.

Only there was a problem.

In those days, the church included both Hellenists and Hebrews. Both were Jewish Christians, but the Hellenists had broader connections outside Palestine, had adopted many

Greek customs, and spoke Greek as their main language. The Hebrews were mainly Palestinian Jews who spoke Aramaic. United in Christ, they formed one body, but when it came to the daily distribution of food, the Hellenists complained against the Hebrews that their widows were being overlooked.

The problem could not be solved by encouraging the widows to take personal action by budgeting more carefully and practicing better self-care. The system itself needed to change so that each widow would be treated fairly regardless of her language and culture. Wisely, the Hebrew leadership responded to make the necessary changes, honoring their core commitments and enlisting the gifts of others.

> And the twelve called together the whole community of the disciples and said, "It is not right that we should neglect the word of God in order to wait on tables. Therefore, friends, select from among yourselves seven men of good standing, full of the Spirit and of wisdom, whom we may appoint to this task, while we, for our part, will devote ourselves to prayer and to serving the word." What they said pleased the whole community, and they chose Stephen, a man full of faith and the Holy Spirit, together with Philip, Prochorus, Nicanor, Timon, Parmenas, and Nicolaus, a proselyte of Antioch. (Acts 6:2-5)

Instead of responding defensively, or offering excuses, or trying to justify the situation, the twelve found a solution that the whole community could approve. Instead of dividing their attention between serving the Word and serving the daily distribution, they would focus on the Word and appoint new leaders who could give their full attention to the distribution. In addition, in contrast to the twelve who were Hebrew, the seven new leaders were all Hellenists, as indicated by the listed names. Justice would now be done—and would be seen to be done—by a visibly expanded leadership.

Today we have our own social and structural issues to address. Around the globe, women still suffer from neglect and injustice. They face discrimination, sexual assault and other forms of violence, and a lack of food, clean water, healthcare, and other resources. In Canada, over the last thirty years, nearly twelve hundred Indigenous women have gone missing or been murdered. While Indigenous women make up just 4 percent of the population, they account for 12 percent of missing women and 16 percent of murdered women in the country.[1] In the United States, both the historical record and up-to-the-minute news reports chronicle instances of racial injustice and race-based violence.[2] In Christian circles, yet another conference featured an all-white list of speakers, and when the conference was canceled because of low registration, those who had questioned the lack of diversity were blamed.[3] Where is the justice done and seen to be done?

As in the time of Moses and in the early church, we need social and structural change. We may not have the power of Moses to singlehandedly change the system, or the collective power of the twelve apostles to restructure a community. But we need the practical wisdom of Jethro and the openness of Moses to listen. We need the nondefensive posture and willingness to act that was shown by the early leaders of the

1. Daniel LeBlanc, "List of Missing, Killed Aboriginal Women Involves 1,200 Cases," *Globe and Mail*, May 1, 2014, https://www.theglobeandmail.com/news/national/rcmp-dont-deny-report-of-more-than-1000-murdered-missing-native-women/article18363451/.
2. For more on the church, racial injustice, and white supremacy, see, among others, Drew G. I. Hart, *Trouble I've Seen: Changing the Way the Church Views Racism* (Harrisonburg, VA: Herald Press, 2016).
3. Kathy Khang, "No Justice, No Peace of the Gospel Conference," October 26, 2017, http://www.kathykhang.com/2017/10/26/no-justice-no-peace-gospel-conference/.

church. We need good questions, sustained engagement, ongoing action, and vigorous prayer.

Yet in our day, a high interest in self-care seems to move in the opposite direction toward disengagement, withdrawal, and focusing on one's self to the exclusion of larger social concerns. As one keen observer notes:

> Self-care seems to mean anything and everything: if an activity (or inactivity) makes you feel better, in body or mind, then it's self-care. It could be yoga or cooking or simply turning off the news. . . . It's nice to think that our bubble baths and personal time might have a larger political purpose . . . but more often than not, our acts of self-care are simply acts of privilege. Rather than being a route to social change, self-care has become a destination in itself.[4]

Dismantling racism and sexism, ending poverty, and addressing other social ills requires ongoing work, determination, prayer, and yes, self-care. We need self-care that genuinely cares for ourselves and our deepest needs without isolating us from the needs of others. We need self-care that refreshes and validates us for our work in the world without it becoming our permanent destination. We need self-care that can both comfort us when the way is hard *and* empower us to live with compassion and perseverance.

What concerns do you have for social and structural change in our world and in your own life? In what ways does self-care empower you to engage these?

---

4. Arwa Mahdawi, "Generation Treat Yo'self: The Problem with 'Self-Care,'" *The Guardian*, January 12, 2017, https://www.theguardian.com/lifeandstyle/2017/jan/12/self-care-problems-solange-knowles.

THE GIFT OF SELF-CARE: KNOW YOUR LIMITS

When I'm feeling battered by the news of yet another instance of racial violence, I might need to give myself grace to escape and turn off the news for a while. I might treat myself to an evening of art or music as a way of saying yes, the world is still beautiful, yes, my life and the lives of those around me still matter. Such moments can't solve the challenges in our world today, and they're no substitute for needed change, but they can offer some respite and allow time to recharge.

- **REFLECT** on where you may be struggling against systemic social structures. The weariness you feel may be because of these larger forces and their resistance to change. Do what you can, but know your limits. Give yourself grace. Avoid burnout by taking breaks before exhaustion sets in. Know that the Spirit of God continues to work even as you rest.

- **REACH OUT** to others when you need help. Like Moses, are you engaged in work that's simply too big for one person? What might others do to help you? Who might join you and appreciate the opportunity to share their gifts? Know your own limits and ask for help while also respecting the limits and boundaries of others.

- **WHAT FORMS** of self-care refresh you from the rigors of daily life and empower you to go on? Take good care of yourself not as an end in itself but as an act of refreshment and engagement.

4

Heart to Heart

We were made for relationships.
—RICK WARREN

At a recent funeral, a grandson gave a moving tribute to his ninety-four-year-old grandfather. Once a week as often as they were able, the two would meet for breakfast at a local restaurant. Over eggs and bacon, they talked sports, they talked life, and they sometimes fell silent and simply rested in their relationship. Even when the grandson had a son of his own, and then a second son, their weekly breakfasts continued, and he would often bring the children, who loved to stir the cream into great-grandpa's coffee.

Now in his mid-thirties, the grandson spoke of how grateful he felt at having his grandfather in his life for so many years. People would say to him, "That's such a nice thing that you're doing for your grandfather, to have breakfast with him."

"No," he would say, "this isn't something that I'm doing *for* him. I want to have our breakfast every week as often as we can make it, and now I have the privilege of sharing my grandfather with my own sons too."

For him, the weekly breakfasts with Grandpa were actually a form of self-care. He could share whatever was on his mind as he changed jobs, got married, and had children of his own. And theirs was a mutual relationship, as he witnessed his grandfather adjust to being a widower, sell his house to move into a condo, give up driving, and allow his grandson to start picking him up for their breakfasts together. For both grandson and grandfather, self-care and caring for one another came together in a beautiful way.

CARING TIMES TWO

As a young woman, Mary had a promising future. She had a large extended family, and she looked forward to having children of her own someday. She was engaged to be married to a man well known to her family—to Joseph, who was both a man of faith and a steady worker who would be a good provider. For Mary, the road ahead seemed clear, and she could walk into the future with happy anticipation.

Until Mary's world turned upside down.

On that day an angel appeared to Mary, and if the sudden presence of an angel wasn't terrifying enough, the angel announced that she would have a son. Before she married Joseph. By the Holy Spirit. A son who would be the holy Son of God. A king who would reign forever. The angel announced all this as good news, as a sign of God's favor, but it must have flooded the young woman's mind and heart with sudden dread.

How could Mary possibly have a child before her marriage to Joseph? Would Joseph even believe that she had been faithful to him? What would her family say? How could she give birth to the Son of God? What kind of king could reign forever? And why had she been chosen? Mary was troubled by the angel's announcement and full of questions.

Once the angel left, Mary packed her bags and literally headed for the hills to visit her relative Elizabeth. For Mary, self-care meant both withdrawing from life as usual and reaching out to someone for support. Instead of struggling alone with her questions, instead of feeling overwhelmed and isolated by what was to come, Mary turned to the one person whom she thought might understand what she was going through.

Despite their difference in age, Mary and Elizabeth had a lot in common and could care for one another as they cared for themselves. Both had a story to tell about the sudden visit of an angel, for Gabriel had come both to Mary and to Elizabeth's husband, Zechariah. Both had been surprised by God. Both now expected a miraculous birth. They had so much to share that Mary extended her stay for about the next three months.

I'm not sure that I would have stayed so long even if I needed someone to talk to. With today's technology, I'm much more likely to phone or email family and friends at a distance than to invite myself over for a few months. But Mary apparently found comfort and energy in her extended visit with Elizabeth.

Depending on your personality, you may find that the people in your life affect your self-care in different ways. You might thrive and feel well cared for amid a crowd, or you might prefer to focus one-on-one. You might love to be with people every night of the week, or thrive and feel well cared for when you can spend that time alone. Everyone is different—extrovert, introvert, ambivert. None of these categories is absolute, or right or wrong, or better or worse than another. But how you respond to social stimulation can help you discern how much and in what ways other people might affect your self-care.

In what ways has your relationship with family or friends meant a mutual caring for one another? Are you able to ask for help when you need it? How does your tendency toward more extroversion or introversion influence your self-care choices?

CLOSE TO THE HEART OF GOD

While Mary's troubled spirit and her many questions had sent her running to Elizabeth, she ran also to the God of Scripture for comfort, strength, and inspiration. Even though her life had taken a wholly unexpected turn, even with all her turmoil and questions, Mary gave voice to a song of praise.

Mary's song grew out of the long history and faith of her people, echoing the song of Hannah, who gave thanks to God for her son, Samuel, and drawing on the Psalms and other portions of Scripture. As Mary pondered these in her heart, she found the answers to some of her questions. What kind of king would her son be? Mighty and merciful, a king who would turn the world upside down just as God had upended her own life, a king who would bring down the proud and powerful to lift up the lowly, satisfy the hungry, and send the rich away with nothing. Why had God chosen her? As a sign of God's favor just as the angel had said, to be a blessing to all generations.

I'm touched by Mary's intimacy with Scripture and with the God who had chosen her. Although Elizabeth must have been a significant support, and although Joseph would follow through with their wedding plans, Mary's hope and heart ultimately rested in God her Savior. Mary took care of herself by withdrawing from her usual surroundings. She and Elizabeth took care of one another as they spent time together. Most of all, Mary received God's care through Scripture, song, and God's sure presence.

While in prison, the apostle Paul also relied heavily on the support of others and on his relationship with God. At the end of his second letter to Timothy, he described how only Luke remained with him, and he asked Timothy to join them. With characteristic boldness—given both Paul's personality and their close relationship as mentor and mentee—Paul outlined for Timothy exactly what he needed: "Do your best to come to me soon. . . . Get Mark and bring him with you. . . . When you come, bring the cloak that I left with Carpus at Troas, also the books, and above all the parchments" (2 Timothy 4:9-13).

Paul was well able to tell Timothy what he needed, confident that Timothy would do his best. But he also knew the limits of what others could do for him. He had already sent some of his coworkers to serve in other areas. He knew that some of his former supporters had deserted him or actively worked against him. He had been alone to make his first defense before the authorities.

Yet Paul did not give up hope, for he said, "The Lord stood by me and gave me strength" (2 Timothy 4:17). When others could not—or would not—be with him, Paul could rely on the God who had called him and transformed his life. Through every trial of shipwreck, beatings, betrayal, imprisonment, and other hardships, God had carried him through and would see him through to the end. Like Mary, Paul depended on God's care: "The Lord will rescue me from every evil attack and save me for his heavenly kingdom. To him be the glory forever and ever. Amen" (2 Timothy 4:18).

Research today indicates that prayer can play a significant role in maintaining our mental, emotional, physical, and spiritual health.[1] How has prayer been part of your self-care?

RUNNING TO JESUS

Early in my ministry, I met regularly with one of our denominational leaders. When I was troubled, he listened and would pray with me. When I had questions, instead of giving me the answer, which is what I was looking for, he helped me think through the issues and options for myself. Best of all, I remember his counsel in times of difficulty: "When you feel like running, then run to Jesus."

---

1. Elizabeth Pessin, "Prayer Improves Health," *Huffington Post*, January 20, 2017, https://www.huffingtonpost.com/elizabeth-pessin/prayer-improves-health_b_9018194.html.

No relative or spouse, mentor or friend can be with us at all times and in all circumstances, to say and do just the right thing every time. But we can always run to Jesus and find that God is faithful: "It is of the Lord's mercies that we are not consumed, because his compassions fail not. They are new every morning: great is thy faithfulness. The Lord is my portion, saith my soul; therefore will I hope in him" (Lamentations 3:22-24 KJV).

Even when life is hard—when we feel overwhelmed by too much bad news in the world, or too much upheaval in our personal lives, or the swirl of our own anxiety over things real or imagined—we will not be consumed by these things. God's mercies and compassions never fail.

I love the plural forms here, for they remind me that God's mercies and compassions are never just one thing for one time—they are many and various and forever. And I love the irony—"the Lord is my portion" refers back to the Promised Land where instead of land, Aaron received the Lord as his "portion" (see Numbers 18:20). Only, God wasn't a portion—without land of his own, Aaron would depend on the Lord for everything.

I'm learning that lesson too.

When my husband was first told that he had cancer, his doctor said, "You have a good chance at a cure." I kept repeating the words over and over in my head. The words *good* and *cure* sounded hopeful, as if I could pray for healing and God would graciously answer yes. But the word *chance* made me nervous, as if life now hung in the balance, ready to fall apart or hang together despite my prayers or anything else we might do.

We waited for further testing . . . we waited to speak to an oncologist . . . and then we waited for surgery. I could bear the waiting, for waiting meant that nothing terrible had happened yet. The rest of our lives seemed to go on as usual. "This is just a blip," my husband said. But still I worried. What would become of us? How could I take care of my husband come what may? And who would take care of me?

Yes, I had friends, family, and a church community I knew would rally round us. Yes, my husband had excellent medical care thanks to the Canadian health system. Yes, I tried to practice good self-care, eating right and taking time to de-stress. But at a deeper level, as in Scripture, God's care became my portion and my everything.

Early one morning, in that liminal space between sleep and full consciousness, I heard a voice: "Whatever happens, everything will be all right, because I'm going to take care of you both." Suddenly I was wide awake, as startled as Mary might have been at the sight of the angel Gabriel. The voice was not my husband's, since he continued to sleep peacefully beside me. I'm quite sure it wasn't my own subconscious, for my subconscious mind tends more toward worry than reassurance. At the risk of being presumptuous, or hopelessly naïve, or sounding like a lunatic, I wanted to say with Eli the priest and the disciple whom Jesus loved and all the saints throughout history: "It is the Lord!"

My husband was right that his cancer turned out to be "just a blip." His surgery went well, he needed no further treatment, and in due course he returned to work, running, and daily living. But many times since then, through various trials and the stresses common to human life, I have returned to those incredible words of care. When all my self-care strategies fail, when I fail myself and others, when those closest to me have done their best yet still leave me wanting for more, God remains forever faithful: "Whatever happens, everything will be all right, because I'm going to take care of you both."

In Scripture and in our lives today, God's care may be evident through an angel or audible word, through Scripture and prayer, through a miraculous healing, or through some other direct intervention. At other times, God's care may be mediated to us by family, friends, medical professionals, or some other means. In what ways have you experienced God's care?

THE GIFT OF SELF-CARE: CULTIVATE FRIENDSHIP

In my search for self-care, I'm discovering that the best self-care is not just about me. Family, friendships, and other mutual relationships of caring play important roles, and God's ongoing and ever-faithful care sustains my life, my self-care, and everything. So while friendships with others and friendship with God have immeasurable worth for their own sake, they also contribute powerfully to self-care.

Yet loneliness is a growing health concern. In the United States, the former surgeon general Vivek H. Murthy writes: "We live in the most technologically connected age in the history of civilization, yet rates of loneliness have doubled since the 1980s. Today, over 40 percent of adults in America report feeling lonely, and research suggests that the real number may well be higher."[2]

For older adults, social interaction may become more limited because of the death of a spouse, the loss of friends, ill health, and more limited mobility. Yet loneliness is not only a challenge of aging. In his article, Murthy focuses his remarks on loneliness in the workplace. In my part of the world, the Vancouver Foundation reports that 30 percent of young adults ages eighteen to twenty-four say that they are lonely "almost always" or "often."[3]

Expanding our network of relationships is one way to deal with loneliness.

- **CULTIVATE MUTUAL RELATIONSHIPS.** Make friends with your family. Have a heart-to-heart talk with a friend. If you're lonely, consider inviting a neighbor to join you for a walk or a cup of coffee. Be aware of the people in your workplace, church, community center, or wherever you go, and make a new friend. Real relationships take time, so slow down, listen, and find common ground and interests. Ralph Waldo Emerson was right: "The only way to have a friend is to be one."

- **CULTIVATE FRIENDSHIP WITH GOD.** "I have called you friends," Jesus said to his disciples (John 15:15). But what does it mean for us to be friends with God? Part II of

2. Vivek H. Murthy, "Work and the Loneliness Epidemic," *Harvard Business Review*, September 2017, https://hbr.org/cover-story/2017/09/work-and-the-loneliness-epidemic.
3. Vancouver Foundation, *Connect and Engage: A Survey of Metro Vancouver*, November 2017, 3, https://www.vancouverfoundation.ca/sites/all/themes/connengage/files/VF-Connect-Engage-report.pdf.

this book gives special attention to spending time with God in prayer, Scripture, Sabbath, lament, and bearing fruit.

■ **IF WORKING AT RELATIONSHIPS** sounds too busy to be self-care, give yourself permission to take a sacred pause. Rest in the knowledge that God is with you.

Part II

S O U L

5

Tending Your Soul

You only need a tiny scrap of time to move toward God.
—*THE CLOUD OF UNKNOWING*, TRANS. BERNARD BANGLEY

In Lewis Carroll's *Through the Looking-Glass, and What Alice Found There*, Alice disagrees with Humpty Dumpty's use of the word *glory* to mean "a nice knock-down argument."

But "glory" doesn't mean "a nice knock-down argument," Alice objected.

"When *I* use a word," Humpty Dumpty said in rather a scornful tone, "it means just what I choose it to mean—neither more nor less."

"The question is," said Alice, "whether you *can* make words mean so many different things."

"The question is," said Humpty Dumpty, "which is to be master—that's all."[1]

---

1. Lewis Carroll, *Through the Looking-Glass, and What Alice Found There* (Philadelphia: Henry Altemus, 1897), 123, https://books.google.com/books?id=i2MCAAAAYAAJ. First published 1871.

Alice and Humpty Dumpty might just as well have been arguing over the word *soul*, for the word appears to mean so many different things. In Scripture, the basic meaning of the soul is to have life, and the same word is translated variously into English as soul, inner self, spirit, desire, heart, person, living being. *Soul* is used to describe both people and animals, both mind and will. It can stand for one's inner emotional life and for the whole person. The word has multiple meanings. It's almost as if the word can mean just what you choose it to mean.

These multiple meanings make it impossible to sharply define the soul. In fact, the words *heart* and *soul* are both used in Scripture to talk about the center of our being. And in the general sense of having life, *soul* can include heart, mind, strength, and more. For those like Alice who want words to mean just one thing, the soul can be confusing!

Yet the fluid nature of the word reminds us that life itself cannot be sharply defined and neatly compartmentalized into different sections. When Jesus says love God with all your heart and with all your soul and with all your mind and with all your strength, the main point isn't to identify four distinctly different gifts but to embrace all of life.

What affects our inner life affects our outer life. What feeds our minds influences our emotions. How we feel physically marks our whole being. The overlap in meaning between heart, soul, mind, and strength mirrors this overlap in our experience. So too in our self-care. While I use *heart* to represent the center of our well-being and *soul* to represent our spiritual well-being, the two gifts overlap. Both are directed God-ward, both involve prayer, and both are grounded in Scripture. These common themes will appear again and again, linking together heart, soul, mind, and strength.

SACRED PAUSES

Five years ago, I wrote a book on spiritual practice because I needed it. In some ways, I had been writing that book my whole life. As a child, I learned the table grace, "Come, Lord Jesus, be our guest, and let this food to us be blest." As a high school student, I memorized long passages of Scripture, including the entire book of 1 John. As an adult, I continued to value Scripture and prayer, and I also experimented with fasting, Sabbath keeping, and other practices.

So when my father-in-law was diagnosed with a brain tumor and told to get his affairs in order, and when at the same time both my mother-in-law and my mother were in poor health and needing care, and as I continued to lead and serve my congregation, I knew that I also needed to care for my own inner life. With the pressure of many responsibilities and a weariness of soul, I needed to be refreshed and renewed, to remain grounded and sustained by God's Spirit.

I found that in sacred pauses throughout my day. Instead of waiting for a day off to shed my weariness and recharge, and instead of waiting for a week's vacation to get away, I drew near to God each day and found that God indeed drew near to me. Those daily sacred pauses refreshed me—a snatch of prayer while waiting in line at the grocery store, a few moments at the piano while waiting for the pasta to be done, a walk around the block with a verse of Scripture, writing in my journal. Yes, I still needed days off and times to get away, but in between I found God's renewal in sacred pauses every day. Over time, what I was learning became a book: *Sacred Pauses: Spiritual Practices for Personal Renewal*.

I needed sacred pauses five years ago, and I still do today. I'm still practicing, because I still need to slow down and draw near to God in various ways. I still need to be nourished by spiritual practice. "Prayer and spirituality are part of self-care at a deeper level," says a friend of mine who also teaches practical theology. In other words, prayer, Scripture, and other spiritual practices can deepen self-care to our very souls.

What spiritual practices have contributed to your self-care? Are there some practices that you would like to try?

LISTENING FOR GOD IN PRAYER

For worship one Sunday morning, I read our designated Scripture, which outlined Jesus' double commandment to love God and love our neighbor. I had read the text many times before, alone and in the congregation. I had preached on it and heard many sermons on what Jesus called the most important commandment. Only this time, the words came alive to me in a new way.

> One of the teachers of religious law was standing there listening to the debate. He realized that Jesus had answered well, so he asked, "Of all the commandments, which is the most important?"
>
> Jesus replied, "The most important commandment is this: 'Listen, O Israel! The Lord our God is the one and only

Lord. And you must love the Lord your God with all your heart, all your soul, all your mind, and all your strength.' The second is equally important: 'Love your neighbor as yourself.' No other commandment is greater than these." (Mark 12:28-31 NLT)

Suddenly, I realized that the most important commandment from Jesus begins with an important prerequisite: "Listen!"

I was so struck by the force of the word that I almost stopped reading in the middle of worship. If we are to love God, we need to *listen*. If we are to love our neighbor as ourselves, we need to *listen*. As far as great commandments go, listening ranks right up there with loving. Listening and loving go together.

In our rush to do good, we sometimes forget that, don't we? At least I do. If there's a problem in my life or in the church or in the world at large, I want to fix it. I want to tweet out my protest against racism and sexual harassment, to blog about employment practices to promote reform in the church. I want to lean in, speak up, and take action. Like the prophet Micah, in my own small way, I want to do justice and love kindness—and I need to remember that he added "walk humbly with your God" (Micah 6:8). That means I also need to listen, and if I take the words of Jesus seriously, I need to listen even before I spring into action—to listen as God speaks through Scripture, in the life of Jesus, to my own heart and soul, and in and through others.

"The essential thing is not what we say but what God says to us and through us," wrote Mother Teresa.[2] Yet how

---

2. Mother Teresa, *In the Heart of the World: Thoughts, Stories, and Prayers*, ed. Becky Benenate (Novato, CA: New World Library, 1997), 20.

often my and our prayers begin with a torrent of words, filled with praise, adoration, thanks, confession, doubt, questions, lament, blessing, and always asking, asking, asking.

There's nothing wrong with any of that. The book of Psalms includes many prayers asking for God's help, forgiveness, deliverance, protection, and guidance. Jesus himself encourages his followers to pray both for their personal needs and for God's will, to be persistent in praying for justice, to keep on asking, seeking, and knocking. The letter to the Philippians instructs readers "*in everything* by prayer and supplication with thanksgiving let your requests be made known to God" (Philippians 4:6, emphasis added). Prayer as talking to God and asking for help can be a vital part of a healthy relationship with God and healthy soul care.

But it's just one part.

A one-sided barrage of words falls short of conversation and real relationship, which require give and take, asking and receiving, speaking and listening. If I'm doing all the talking with my husband and with my friends, if I never give them a chance to speak their minds and their hearts, our communication and relationship suffer and become unhealthy. So too, if I long for friendship with God. I need to take time to become quiet. I need to practice prayer not only as talking *to* God but as hearing *from* God as well.

In silent, centering prayer, I sit quietly, breathe slowly, and turn my thoughts toward God—the Creator, Redeemer, Sustainer of all things, the one revealed in Jesus Christ as God with us by the Holy Spirit. Some forms of centering prayer focus on clearing one's mind and heart, or emptying oneself—I do that too in the sense of suspending the day's agenda for a time and setting aside distractions. But instead of becoming empty, I think of centering prayer as silent prayer that centers me on God. Instead of asking for one more thing, instead of pouring out my thoughts and fears, I rest in God's love and care, and I listen.

I don't usually hear an audible voice, or see an angel as Mary, the mother of Jesus, saw the angel Gabriel. But sometimes a word of Scripture comes to mind. Sometimes I'm prompted to pray for a particular situation, or to reach out to someone in some way. Sometimes the silence itself seems healing, an oasis amid a noisy and demanding world. "For God alone my soul waits in silence," says the psalmist, "from him comes my salvation. He alone is my rock and my salvation, my fortress; I shall never be shaken" (Psalm 62:1-2).

Research suggests that silence can lower blood pressure, relieve stress, boost creativity, and even allow our bodies to develop new brain cells.[3]
How much silence do you experience in a typical day?
In what ways do you wait for God in silence?

LISTENING FOR GOD IN SCRIPTURE

When I listen for God in Scripture, I also begin with silence. I turn off my devices, tune out the background noise, and come to the Word expecting to hear from God. That silent

---

3. Daniel A. Gross, "This Is Your Brain on Silence," *Nautilus* 38, July 7, 2016, http://nautil .us/issue/38/noise/this-is-your-brain-on-silence-rp.

expectation is the first step in the ancient practice of *lectio divina*, or "divine reading" of Scripture.

Then I read the text slowly and prayerfully, most often aloud, as people did in the ancient world. On the first reading, I get a sense of the entire passage and notice where God directs my attention. On the second reading, I dwell on the particular word or phrase on which my attention rests. On the third reading, I ask how this word or phrase speaks into my life today. I sit with that thought awhile, give thanks for God's leading, and move into my day, holding the Word I've received and seeking to live it out.

This movement—through silence, reading, dwelling, listening, and living into the Word—has been a powerful practice in my life. It's not a magic formula, and it doesn't automatically "work" every time. But it immerses me in Scripture and puts me in the posture of listening for God. It strengthens my faith and communicates God's care, protection, and guidance. Like prayer, reading Scripture in this way is soul care and self-care.

Last year I was invited to introduce *lectio divina* as part of an adult formation class in another church. After outlining the basics, I invited everyone to sit comfortably, close their eyes if they wished, and enter into a time of silence and anticipation of listening for God. "First listen to the psalm and notice where God draws your attention," I said, and then I read Psalm 121. After a moment of silence, I asked, "What word or phrase are you drawn to?" I then read the psalm again. After another brief silence, I asked, "How does this word or phrase speak into your life?" I then read the psalm a third time.

As we concluded our *lectio divina*, I asked if anyone would like to share what they had heard. One had been most drawn to the opening line, "I lift up my eyes to the hills." Another had noticed the all-encompassing nature of God's care "by day" and "by night." Another shared a personal decision she faced and the reassurance she felt from the end of the psalm that God would keep her "from this time on and forevermore."

Each experience of listening for God in the psalm was different and personal and expressed God's care for each of us in our own particular circumstances. And practicing *lectio divina* together added a new dimension of God's care as we gathered around the same text, yet heard and understood it somewhat differently, in ways that enriched its meaning and power as we shared together.

In what ways has Scripture contributed to your self-care?
Have you experienced lectio divina *alone or with a group?*

THE GIFT OF SELF-CARE: FEED YOUR SOUL

Both silent prayer and *lectio divina* are ancient ways of listening for God and seeking God's friendship—methods practiced by Christians for centuries and part of a living tradition even today. In their capacity to move us toward God, these practices nourish our inner being, feed our souls, and thus contribute to our self-care.

We can listen for God and feed our souls in other ways as well. "Looking at art is one way of listening to God," says nun

and art historian Wendy Beckett.[4] And I might add to the list
activities such as painting, reading a good book, listening to
music, playing an instrument, spending time in solitude, taking
a nap, singing, walking in the rain, coloring with a child, playing with a kitten, and much more.

- **DRAW UP** your own list of practices that feed your soul.
  Some might seem more traditional, like Bible study or
  praying the Lord's Prayer. Other practices might seem less
  obviously connected to your soul, like listening to your
  favorite podcast. Feel free to start with one or more of the
  things I've already mentioned as a springboard for your
  own ideas, or build an entirely new list from scratch. Just
  as each person's experience with *lectio divina* is unique, so
  the things that feed our souls may well vary from person
  to person.

- **TAKE TIME** to feed your soul with one of the practices
  from your list. Think of it as a sacred pause, whether it's
  a few moments to read some poetry, a Sunday morning
  for worship and building community, or a solo weekend
  retreat in the mountains. The beauty of a pause is that it
  can be as short or as long as needed.

- **SIT IN SILENCE** for five minutes, and listen. Listen to
  the sounds around you—a ticking clock, the sound of the
  refrigerator, the rise and fall of your own breath. Let these
  sounds gradually fall away as you listen underneath them

---

4. Wendy Beckett, epigraph to *A Child's Book of Prayer in Art* (New York: DK Publishing,
1995).

and around them for the cry of your own heart and soul, for the voice of God.

■ **PRACTICE** *lectio divina* with one of the following passages of Scripture: Psalm 23; Psalm 121; Matthew 5:1-12; Mark 4:35-41; 1 Corinthians 13; or choose your own text.

■ **EVEN IF** you only have a moment or two, remember that it only takes a tiny scrap of time to move toward God, and that time is precious.

6

Sabbath as Soul Care

Most of the days of the week we do what we have to do, what is expected of us. Sabbath keeping frees us to take delight in everything, to uncork our own spontaneity.
—MARVA DAWN

As a budding biblical studies scholar working on his doctorate, my husband would set aside every Sunday as a Sabbath from his studies. No reading. No writing long essays with long footnotes. No rushing off to a class or group study session. No shutting himself away in his little closet of an office in our student apartment. I, too, would set aside my writing. No going to my study carrel in the library. No sitting in front of the computer. We might work day and into the night the rest of the week. But come Sunday, we would take a break.

We'd have a leisurely breakfast, then go to church for worship and to connect with our newfound community of faith. On the first Sunday of the month, we'd usually stay for the carry-in meal, to which everyone brought a dish to share, as well as personal plates and cutlery so no one had to stay to wash up. Other Sundays we would often go to someone's home, and the rest of the day we'd see friends, or go for a walk, or just hang out on our own. For a treat, we'd borrow a television from the seminary audiovisual department so we could watch college basketball games, which we had come to love since living in Indiana and Virginia. I guess that might qualify as "work," since it meant my husband making the trek across campus on foot and lugging the TV back and up two flights of stairs to our apartment! But besides making our meals, that was about the only work we'd do on our student Sabbaths.

Of course there were exceptions—like when one of my husband's comprehensive exams fell on a Monday. In that case he postponed Sabbath to study on the Sunday before. But for the most part, we said no to our work and being productive, in favor of saying yes to self-care as soul care, yes to worship, and yes to community. We said no to the mall and consumerism, both to honor the Sabbath and because as students we didn't have much money anyway. We said yes to hospitality, although as newcomers to the city and seminary community, we were more often on the receiving end. We said yes to recognizing our own limits and yes to God's sovereignty and ongoing work in our lives. Everything did *not* depend on us; instead, we depended on God. Sabbath as self-care meant rest, celebration, fun, and freedom.

FLASH FORWARD

Today my Sunday has become a workday. I'm often up early, putting the finishing touches on my sermon or catching up on emails that I didn't get to during the week. Just as often, I'm up late writing on Sunday nights so I have a new blog post for Monday mornings. Thankfully though, I still avoid the mall, we still stay for potluck meals, and worship is still worship. Often when I close my eyes and sing out my praise and lament, I forget about the rest of the congregation, and when the music ends and I open my eyes, I'm almost surprised that everyone is there. For me, that's a Sabbath moment. Yet the once-a-week, all-day Sabbath of our student years has otherwise disappeared.

I know I'm not alone in missing Sabbath. For many people, working on Sundays has become commonplace. Besides pastors and other religious workers, consider doctors, nurses, and other hospital staff . . . caregivers in homes preparing meals, cleaning, or performing other duties . . . police and firefighters, emergency dispatchers, air traffic controllers . . . farm workers, restaurant workers, grocery and other retail clerks, baristas, and many more.

Even those not technically working on a Sunday say that finding a whole Sabbath day remains a challenge. Just ask the church secretary who worships in her own congregation and finds herself constantly asked about bulletin announcements, or where to find the dry erase markers for the whiteboard, or how to unjam the photocopier. Or the member of the nominations committee who spends his Sunday morning time in the church foyer seeking out and talking to potential nominees.

Or the young mom whose husband is working, yet she gets herself, their three children, and all their related books, snacks, and diapers ready for church and out the door in the morning.

Sometimes church can feel more like work than Sabbath. Yet skipping it doesn't automatically resolve the challenges: with the busyness of the kids' hockey games, soccer tournaments, or swim meets that often take place on Sundays . . . the pull of the mall to pick up a forgotten item or to get a head start on the week . . . the ever-present beep of another work-related text or email even on the weekend, even on a holiday.

All this leaves me longing for the Sabbath days that my husband and I once enjoyed together. Were they really as idyllic as I remember them? Or has my longing softened the edges and made the Sabbath more ideal than real? If so, at least that ideal is shared by others searching for a more human and humane pace of life. As theologian and author Marva Dawn describes the Sabbath,

> most of the days of the week we do what we have to do, what is expected of us. Sabbath keeping frees us to take delight in everything, to uncork our own spontaneity. Because there is nothing we *have* to do, we are free suddenly to say yes to invitations, to read fairy tales, to be children, to discover the presence of God hidden all around us. To keep the Sabbath invites us to have festival fun, to play, to enjoy our guests and our activities, to relish the opportunity for worship, to celebrate the eternal presence of God himself. We feast in every aspect of our being—physical, intellectual, social, emotional, spiritual—and we feast with music, beauty, food, and affection. Our bodies, minds, souls, and spirits celebrate together with others that God is in our midst.[1]

1. Marva Dawn, *Keeping the Sabbath Wholly: Ceasing, Resting, Embracing, Feasting* (Grand Rapids, MI: William B. Eerdmans, 1989), 202.

SABBATH AS SOUL CARE

*In what ways has a weekly Sabbath been a
part of your life? How has your experience
of Sabbath changed over time?*

A HUMAN PACE OF LIFE

As I search the Scriptures, I find plenty of evidence for this
more human pace of life as part of Sabbath keeping. From the
beginning, God demonstrated both work and rest, and gifted
the people with that same rhythm as part of the religious law
that became a vital mark of identity and community for the
Hebrew people. As gifts embedded in creation itself, work
meant acknowledging God in six days of labor and creativity,
and Sabbath meant acknowledging God with a seventh day of
worship and ceasing from work. The Sabbath meant refreshment and renewal, a welcome relief from the week's labor, and
a joyous expression of trust in God.

Resting from work on the weekly Sabbath stood in contrast
to the relentless, driving productivity of slave labor that the
Hebrew people had experienced in captivity, and it stands in
contrast to the often frenetic pace of our lives today. "You see
all the names of professors along this hallway?" asked a professor friend, gesturing down the corridor of faculty offices.
"Half of them—or maybe more—are divorced." Too many
books to read, too many papers to write, and too little time
meant too much pressure. Combined with high expectations—
both their own and others'—plus a competitive atmosphere
and the politics of academia, the pressures of academic life put
pressure on marriage and family life too.

Would taking a weekly Sabbath have made a difference to these professors and their families? The Sabbath is no cure-all for vocational or marital distress. Yet I can't help but think that more soul care and a more human pace of life might have helped. As Walter Brueggemann notes, "We used to sing the hymn 'Take Time to Be Holy.' But perhaps we should be singing, 'Take time to be human.' Or finally, 'Take time.' Sabbath is taking time . . . time to be holy . . . time to be human."[2]

In Scripture, to be holy means to be set apart. So, for example, the furnishings and utensils of the ancient tabernacle were holy, for they were set apart for use in worship. What would a day set apart for rest look like for you?

A FAMILY SABBATH

For MaryAnn McKibben Dana and her family, life felt overly full, with two careers, two young children, and keeping up with the house and lawn and countless personal and household chores. She and her husband agreed that something needed to change, so they decided on a yearlong experiment to keep a family Sabbath. Taking a day each week to catch their breath seemed like good self-care, but it was also more than that. As they discovered in their own search for a more human pace of life, Dana acknowledges that "the Sabbath isn't really about rest and rejuvenation at its core. That's sometimes a by-product but not the primary purpose. The primary biblical purpose as I see it is to put away the idol of control and power

2. Walter Brueggemann, *Sabbath as Resistance: Saying No to the Culture of Now* (Louisville, KY: Westminster John Knox, 2014), 87.

and a sense that we run the show. We do not. Are we really so very indispensable that we have to be 'on' every single day of our lives except vacation, sickness, and when we just plain crash?"[3]

I agree that the primary purpose of the Sabbath isn't to care for ourselves, yet acknowledging God's power and sovereignty, acknowledging our limits and living within them, reorients our lives in powerfully self-caring ways.

Dana's family experiment demonstrates another difference between Sabbath and self-care as a personal practice: instead of each person developing a personal self-care plan, they explored Sabbath together as a family. Their Sabbath experiment was a family project, and given Dana's pastoral role at the time, it included the cooperation of their church family.

For the Hebrew people, instructions for the Sabbath applied to the entire community—men, women, children, servants, strangers, oxen, donkeys, other livestock—and even to the land. Sabbath was not self-care in the narrow sense of the word but was about more broadly caring for the community and for creation. So when the prophet Isaiah spoke of keeping the Sabbath, he did not focus on personal self-care but broadened that call to the wider community to do good and practice justice (see Isaiah 56:1-2).

Jesus seemed to understand the Sabbath just as broadly. When critics accused his disciples of breaking the Sabbath by picking and eating grain as they walked through a field, Jesus defended them—not in personal terms because they were hungry and needed to eat, but in view of a bigger picture. As

3. MaryAnn McKibben Dana, *Sabbath in the Suburbs: A Family's Experiment with Holy Time* (Atlanta: Chalice Press, 2012), 136.

part of the people's history, David and his companions had eaten bread from the temple that was lawfully to be eaten only by the priests. Technically, they had broken the law, but even Jesus' critics would acknowledge that God had provided for their needs. "The sabbath was made for humankind, and not humankind for the sabbath," Jesus said (Mark 2:27).

When the leaders of the synagogue told the temple crowd that Jesus should confine his miraculous healings to the six-day work week, Jesus called out their hypocrisy: "Does not each of you on the sabbath untie his ox or his donkey from the manger, and lead it away to give it water? And ought not this woman, a daughter of Abraham whom Satan bound for eighteen long years, be set free from this bondage on the sabbath day?" (Luke 13:15-16).

How much more should they show compassion for their fellow human being and sister in the faith! Clearly, for Jesus, Sabbath meant time to exercise human compassion and alleviate suffering just as much as it meant time for worship in the synagogue.

In what ways do you identify with MaryAnn McKibben Dana and her family in their experiment with Sabbath? What challenges do you face that work against taking a day of rest?

THE GIFT OF SELF-CARE: TAKE A WEEKLY SABBATH

Sabbath as self-care sets the tone for a more human pace of life, and it enlarges—dare I say corrects?—our understanding of self-care. Instead of individual soul care, the Sabbath addresses a community of souls in the context of doing good and caring for community and creation.

My current Sabbath practice is a twenty-four-hour social media fast once a week, from six in the evening on Saturday until six in the evening on Sunday. It's not a full technology fast or rest from all work, since I still do emails and use my computer and phone during that time. But even this modified Sabbath practice has created a healthy boundary to the twenty-four-hour-a-day, always-on pull of social media and frees me from screen time in favor of real-life relationships. It reminds me that I don't always have to be "on," that I can let go and let God be God.

It works well for me to have a definite start to my Sabbath on Saturday evening and to continue then at least until Sunday evening, or sometimes Monday morning. That allows me to be deliberate about stopping my social media engagement, instead of vaguely not starting in the morning. And while having an end time in mind helps me to take a full twenty-four-hour Sabbath, I like keeping it somewhat open-ended so that there's no pressure to end my Sabbath at six o'clock on Sunday or any time, so Sabbath flows smoothly back into my ordinary time.

If you'd like to start or renew your Sabbath practice, here are a few suggestions:

- **CHOOSE** a twenty-four-hour period for your Sabbath. If you work or have other commitments on Sundays, choose a different day of the week. You could do it from one evening to the next, as I've been doing, or from morning to morning, or at some other suitable interval.

- **TRY RESTING** from work during that time, or choose a partial fast, like setting aside social media, or not eating out, or staying away from the mall.

- **INSTEAD OF GOING** it alone, talk about Sabbath with your family, roommate, or others to form a communal Sabbath practice.

- **GO TO WORSHIP** without doing church business. If you need to speak with the pastor, to make plans with a council or committee member, or to tend to other business, choose instead to call or email during the week.

- **DO A KINDNESS** for someone else. Speak kindly, visit someone who is shut in, write a letter of condolence or encouragement and mail it.

- **MEET A CLOSE FRIEND** for lunch or coffee. Really listen and share your heart.

- **DO SOMETHING YOU ENJOY.** Go for a day hike, spend the afternoon coloring, eat a meal with your favorite foods.

- **CHOOSE A RITUAL** to start and end your Sabbath practice. Lighting a candle or listening to music can be helpful markers.

- **BE KIND TO YOURSELF** if your Sabbath gets interrupted, or if you decide to break it prematurely. Emergencies can happen. Plans change. God is still God.

7

The Soul's Lament

Trust in him at all times, O people;
pour out your heart before him;
God is a refuge for us.
   —PSALM 62:8

Kim's *Convenience* tells the story of a Korean Canadian couple, their college-aged daughter Janet, their older and estranged son Jung, and their convenience store near downtown Toronto. The award-winning comedy broke new ground as Canada's first television sitcom with Asian actors in leading roles and became the country's number one domestic comedy in its first season.

In one episode, "Appa" tries to comfort his daughter after she finds out that her boyfriend has become engaged to someone else. "Come," Appa says to Janet. "We eat from our sad food group. Starting with cookie dough ice cream. . . . And Cheez Doodles."[1]

I can't say that I have a "sad food group," but I appreciate Appa's response. When your heart gets broken, when your world has fallen apart, when nothing seems to make sense—sometimes you just don't know what to do and can't be comforted by even the most well-meaning words of others. Wisely, Appa doesn't try to explain away his daughter's hurt, or tell her to look on the bright side, or reassure her that she will find someone else. That will come later. But first he shares her grief, and goes for the cookie dough ice cream. They need to lament.

The basic meaning of *lament* is to mourn and express deep grief. Instead of ignoring the pain in life or internalizing it or explaining it away, lament allows us to express our deep feelings. At a funeral, we lament the loss of a loved one with the sharing of memories and tears. Janet and her appa lament the betrayal of her boyfriend with their sad food group. In times of loss and difficulty, our souls need lament as a form of self-care.

WHEN LAMENT IS WHAT YOU NEED

When my professor husband walked into his last Acts class of the semester, his students surprised him with a standing ovation. What a beautiful way to brighten that mid-December afternoon, with a powerful testimony to their good relationship as a class and to his creativity and scholarship, honed over twenty-five years of faithful and effective teaching.

---

1. *Kim's Convenience*, season 2, episode 10, "Janet's Boyfriend," directed by Renuka Jeyapalan, written by Matt Kippen, aired November 28, 2017, on CBC Television.

What the students didn't know, however, and what my husband didn't tell them, was that two days earlier the college president had given him a letter terminating his employment. Not for any fault of his own, he was told, but for "financial reasons." Yet why give him such difficult news right before Christmas when the college wanted him to teach until the end of the next semester? How could the administration justify ending the employment of the only person of color on faculty and hiring a younger, white professor to take his place the following year? And why was he told not to tell anyone beyond his immediate family and "professional advisers"? The personal, legal, moral, and ethical questions weighed on my husband and weighed on me. We didn't have any professional advisers, but we obviously needed them.

I did a lot of lamenting in those days. I lamented my husband's struggle to end well despite the crushing blow he had received. As others learned of his situation, I lamented the impact on other faculty and staff who worried that one day they might also lose their jobs when they turned sixty and Christmas was on the way. I lamented the loss of respect for leadership, the loss of trust, the loss for students.

In my lament, I sought companionship and solace in the Psalms. The book of Psalms is like a hymnal or guide to worship, full of praise for who God is and all that God has done, full of thanksgiving, confession, offering, and yes, even lament. Many psalms reflect a liturgical setting—for ascending to the temple hill and entering its gates, for the crowning and enthronement of kings, for recounting and celebrating God's covenant with the people, for lamenting evil and national disaster as a community.

Other psalms give voice to more personal lament, and during the time of our distress, these spoke to me most deeply.

As the psalmist struggles with those who have wronged him, he cries out:

Give ear to my words, O Lord;
    give heed to my sighing.
Listen to the sound of my cry,
    my King and my God,
    for to you I pray.
O Lord, in the morning you hear my voice;
    in the morning I plead my case to you, and watch.
    (Psalm 5:1-3)

In response to some unspecified trouble, the psalmist expresses this anguish:

I cry aloud to God,
    aloud to God, that he may hear me.
In the day of my trouble I seek the Lord;
    in the night my hand is stretched out without wearying;
    my soul refuses to be comforted.
I think of God, and I moan;
    I meditate, and my spirit faints. *Selah*
You keep my eyelids from closing;
    I am so troubled that I cannot speak. (Psalm 77:1-4)

Although their original context was quite different from my own, the Psalms gave voice to my lament. Across the centuries, from the hillsides and battlefields of Scripture to twenty-first-century suburbia, they spoke to me and for me. Whatever our day of trouble—job loss and other work-related issues, family stress, chronic or unexplained illness, past or present abuse, injustice, violence, war, or other trials—the Psalms allow us to lament. They give us the freedom and the language to speak our pain, anger, and distress, and so promote healing.

Sometimes that pain morphs into complaint and blaming God: "How long, O Lord? Will you forget me forever? How long will you hide your face from me?" (Psalm 13:1). The psalmist questions and accuses:

My God, my God, why have you forsaken me?
    Why are you so far from helping me,
    from the words of my groaning?
O my God, I cry by day, but you do not answer;
    and by night, but find no rest. (Psalm 22:1-2)

Reading complaint after complaint can be exhausting, especially since the Bible contains more psalms of lament than any other genre, accounting for well over a third of the 150 psalms.[2] Even I was beginning to tire of their bitterness and rage. Was the psalmist as innocent and misunderstood as he claimed to be? I wondered. Was everyone around him so deceitful and destructive? Was God to blame for his trials? Did he sometimes exaggerate his difficulties? Do I?

Maybe so. Yet lament still seemed a necessary step toward the psalmist's healing and toward my own—a way to release bad feelings instead of holding them inside where they could do more harm. Besides, as I kept reading the psalms of lament, I came to realize that they move us beyond complaining to something more.

When you need to lament, do you turn to a sad food group? To the Psalms? To something else? How do you express lament?

2. James H. Waltner, *Psalms*, Believers Church Bible Commentary (Scottdale, PA: Herald Press, 2006), 787.

BEYOND COMPLAINT

At the age of thirty-nine, with a wife and two young children, theologian J. Todd Billings learned that he had a rare and incurable form of blood cancer. How could this be? How many more years would he have with his family? What would this mean for his life and faith? He writes,

> In the wake of my own diagnosis and entrance into chemo, I can say that my response was not simple. At times I would cry out in grief to God; along with this, I would lament in protest to God for the sake of my young children. At times I responded in gratitude for—and awe of—all of the gifts that God had already given, even if my life were not to be extended much longer. God is faithful to his promises, and his loving gifts each day are lavish and amazing—and I sometimes sensed that deeply.[3]

In this mix of lament and praise, Billings's journey with cancer reflects the experience of the Psalms, where so often psalms of lament turn out to be psalms of thanksgiving.

So while Psalm 5 begins with sighing and crying out to God, the psalm ends with singing for joy. While Psalm 13 begins with the lament of "How long, O Lord?" it ends with "I will sing to the Lord, because he has dealt bountifully with me." Psalm 22 begins with questioning God's absence, and ends with praise for God's deliverance. For Psalm 77, the sleepless night and day of trouble lead the psalmist to recall God's mighty works.

In Scripture, genuine lament does not exist in a vacuum. It's more than simply complaining and venting bad feelings, for lament moves from deep sorrow to deep trust, from

3. J. Todd Billings, *Rejoicing in Lament: Wrestling with Incurable Cancer and Life in Christ* (Grand Rapids, MI: Brazos Press, 2015), 21.

complaining to confidence in God. As Billings affirms: "We only fully lament when we realize that we're not just expressing ourselves to a human observer but bringing our burdens before the Lord, the Creator, the Almighty, who—in light of our distress—is our Deliverer."[4]

In *Prophetic Lament*, Soong-Chan Rah also points out that "lament is the language of suffering. . . . Lament recognizes the struggles of life and cries out for justice against existing injustices. The status quo is not to be celebrated, but instead must be challenged."[5]

To that end, my husband's lament included advocating for policy changes at the college so no one else would ever have to go through his painful experience. All Canadian human rights provisions should be respected to protect employees from discrimination on the basis of age and race. As in some secular settings, no terminations for "financial reasons" should take place during the Christmas season, and employees over the age of forty should be given a minimum of three weeks to decide on any settlement offer. Whether these and other provisions will be implemented in the future is unknown, but his lament included this cry for justice as a way of caring for others and caring for himself.

In what ways has lament moved you to action?
In what ways has lament deepened your trust
and confidence in God?

---

4. Ibid, 47.
5. Soong-Chan Rah, *Prophetic Lament: A Call for Justice in Troubled Times* (Downers Grove, IL: InterVarsity Press, 2015), 22–23.

STILL TRUSTING

"God doesn't give us more than we can handle." "God has something even better in store for you." "For every closed door, another one will open." When the college terminated my husband's employment, we received these and many more well-meaning comments. I appreciated every kind word, even the ones that we weren't yet ready to hear. I wanted that "something even better," and I longed for that open door that looked to the future even though I couldn't see it. Although we needed to lament, we also needed to hope and trust in God.

Two years later, my husband has now returned to teaching and advising students, this time at the seminary and graduate level. I'm grateful for both the seminary and university that so value his scholarship and expertise that they sought him out and offered new opportunities for ministry. That doesn't change the past with his previous employer, but certainly God has opened other, better doors for him.

I'm aware that doesn't always happen. Somewhere others are struggling, just as pained, and just as loved by God, yet all the doors remain shut. Someone else is receiving bad news with no good way forward. Someone else is still lamenting and still waiting for God to act. Even for us there remain some gaping holes that still need healing, and scars that still sting.

Yet we are humbled by God's grace. When we received more trouble than we could handle, God carried us through. As lament helped us care for ourselves, it also helped us to lean on God, who has proven more than faithful to his promises. So we continue the journey toward healing. We continue to place our trust in God.

*In what ways has God transformed lament
into joy for you? If you are in a season of
lament, how do you hold on to hope?*

THE GIFT OF SELF-CARE: LEARN TO LAMENT

In the Gospels, Jesus reveals himself as a man of sorrows and lament. He weeps at the tomb of his friend Lazarus, who died at home after some days of illness. He laments over the city: "Jerusalem, Jerusalem, the city that kills the prophets and stones those who are sent to it! How often have I desired to gather your children together as a hen gathers her brood under her wings, and you were not willing! See, your house is left to you, desolate. For I tell you, you will not see me again until you say, 'Blessed is the one who comes in the name of the Lord'" (Matthew 23:37-39).

On the cross, Jesus' lament even draws on the Psalms. "My God, my God, why have you forsaken me?" he groans (Matthew 27:46; Mark 15:34). "Into your hands I commit my spirit," he laments as he breathes his last (Luke 23:46 NIV).

Our North American culture may seem more comfortable with success and celebration than with lament.[6] But if we are to practice healthy self-care, we need to care for our whole selves, including those places of hurt and brokenness that cry out for healing. We need to make room for lament.

Gently acknowledge your hurt and brokenness. Whether you bear fresh wounds or have struggled for years, be kind to yourself. Allow yourself to feel bad. Healing can be slow and

---

6. Soong-Chan Rah's *Prophetic Lament* examines this tendency in the American church.

delicate work, especially when it comes to war, racism, child-hood abuse, sexual assault, and other traumatic experiences.

- ■ **EAT** from your "sad food group." Or punch a pillow, write bad poetry, bang on the piano, yell into the wind, stay up half the night venting to your best friend, listen to a sad song, cry. Find a safe way to express your grief and distress. Write an angry letter, then shred or burn it. Go for a hard run, but don't hurt yourself. Avoid drugs, alcohol, and other self-destructive substances and behaviors. If you're raging, don't get behind the wheel of a car. If you're binging, give yourself a time limit. It's one thing to binge-watch Netflix for an afternoon, quite another to do it for an entire week.

- ■ **LET SCRIPTURE GUIDE** your lament to move from complaint to thanksgiving and confidence in God. Read one of the many psalms of personal lament: Psalms 5, 13, 31, 51, 77, 86, 140.

- ■ **CHANNEL YOUR LAMENT** into seeking positive change. Cry out for justice. Challenge the status quo. Find allies, and consult with professional advisers as needed. But know your limits, as we talked about in chapters 2 and 3. Pull back when you need to, and don't feel guilty about it. Know that God is sovereign and at work.

- ■ **IF YOU OR OTHERS ARE CONCERNED** that your soul's lament may be part of a depression, seek help from your doctor, counselor, or other health professional. This is not weakness or cause for self-blame. As we'll see in chapter 11, caring for your mental health is part of good self-care.

8

The Soul and the Fruit of Self-Discipline

Self-discipline is self-caring.
—M. SCOTT PECK

Hello, this is your dental office," said the cheerful voice on the phone. "I'm calling with a reminder that you're overdue to book your next appointment. There's a cancellation for next week if you're able to come in then."

I tried to match the receptionist's cheerful tone with my own as we discussed various dates and finally settled on a mutually agreeable time. But inwardly I was groaning. Going to the dentist has never been my favorite way to spend an hour. So I tend to procrastinate; in fact, I had received a message about my overdue appointment several weeks earlier, one that I had managed to ignore. But there was no avoiding it now. I responded pleasantly as I made the appointment, and silently bribed myself with a post-dentist visit to the library on my way home.

Yet for all my reluctance, seeing the dentist is a basic form of self-care, along with going to the doctor, getting my eyes examined, buying groceries, preparing meals, doing laundry, and a whole host of things that I tend to label as "chores." If self-care is about contributing to my sense of well-being, then these and other chores definitely qualify. Doing laundry means I have fresh towels. Buying groceries means I can bake blueberry scones for breakfast. Going to my dentist and dental hygienist means my teeth get properly cleaned and cared for. All that and more contributes to my sense of well-being.

But that kind of self-care doesn't always feel good in the moment, and it may take some self-discipline to get there.

WHY SELF-CARE DOESN'T ALWAYS FEEL GOOD

Year after year, my beautiful red gloxinia blooms faithfully with huge, velvety, trumpet-shaped flowers. When it's in bloom, I water it almost daily. As the blossoms die off, I pinch them back to encourage more flowers. And when all the flowers are gone, I cut the whole plant down to the soil and move the pot to a cooler part of the house. As the plant rests for the winter, I water it sparingly. When green shoots emerge again in spring, I bring it back from exile into the warmth of the living room, where it will bloom again. The cycle starts over.

I don't find my gloxinia particularly demanding, but helping it flourish does take some care. It's the same with anything else. Whether you're tending a single household plant or an entire garden, a pet or a barnyard, a household or a business, a family or a classroom: taking care of anything requires thoughtful planning and deliberate effort. Even my easygoing gloxinia needs some care. So too, taking care of yourself takes some organization and effort.

If you're already stretched, that effort of self-care might seem like too much. At least that's how it feels to me at times. With an already full schedule and Christmas coming, really the last thing I needed was a trip to the dentist. If I had been thinking, I would have gone in August before my appointment was overdue and before I needed two reminder phone calls. But August had been busy too. Plus, I had definitely preferred spending time in the garden rather than in the dentist's chair!

I don't mean to pick on my dentist, since he, my dental hygienist, and all the staff do great work, but I do feel better about seeing them once my appointment is over. As Dorothy Parker once said, "I hate writing. I love having written." I might say, "I hate going to the dentist. I love having been there." For me, going to the dentist is just not as much fun as an hour in the garden or browsing the new releases at the library. In fact, I'd rather go grocery shopping, do the laundry, or tackle pretty much any other household chore. But I still see my dentist regularly because I know it's good self-care in the long run, that with some effort and a little delayed gratification, it will all be worth it. Good self-care doesn't always have to feel good in the moment.

Some forms of self-care feel better once they're over. We don't enjoy them in the moment, but we're glad that we've done them. What forms of self-care fall into that category for you?

THE NECESSITY AND LIMITS OF SELF-DISCIPLINE

In Scripture, one of the clearest references to self-care includes this appeal to self-discipline. The apostle Paul encourages Timothy, "For this reason I remind you to rekindle the gift of God that is within you through the laying on of my hands; for God did not give us a spirit of cowardice, but rather a spirit of power and of love and of self-discipline" (2 Timothy 1:6-7).

This echoes a portion of an earlier letter: "Do not neglect the gift that is in you, which was given to you through prophecy with the laying on of hands by the council of elders" (1 Timothy 4:14).

I've always wondered why Paul didn't name Timothy's gift more clearly. After all, the other Pauline letters include lists of specific spiritual gifts. Why didn't Paul just choose from among them and speak to Timothy in very specific ways? He could have said, Do not neglect administration. Rekindle your gift of wisdom. Fan into flame your gift of teaching. Be diligent. Instead, he speaks more generally about "your gift" and "the gift of God," which seem so vague.

Perhaps that was Paul's intent, to be deliberately vague so that Timothy would have as much freedom as possible to exercise his gifts as broadly as possible. After all, if Timothy's ministry resembled church work in our context, one day he might be preaching, another day serving at the food bank, another day or afternoon or hour engaged in administration or teaching. For maximum freedom in ministry and maximum effectiveness, different gifts might be called for and exercised at different times. And in each case, it was the gift of God that empowered Timothy for service.

The unspecified language of *gift* might also allow us to imagine ourselves into the text more easily. Whatever Timothy's gifts may have been, whatever gifts we have inside us, Paul's encouragement to Timothy can encourage us today too. Whatever your gifts, don't let them burn out or die out. Don't serve on the edge of exhaustion. Instead, tend your gifts with care. Rekindle them.

The underlying Greek expression in Paul's letter suggests the image of a fire once burning bright and now dying down to embers that need to be rekindled, revived, revitalized. As a young leader in a young and growing church, Timothy might have felt like that fire, once burning bright and now on the edge of burning out. He needed to rekindle his considerable gifts, to revive his energy. In other words, he needed to practice self-care.

To that end, Paul says that God has given us a spirit of power, love, and self-discipline. In some English versions of the Bible, *self-discipline* is translated as "sound mind." If power represents the ability to get things done, if love represents the heart, then self-discipline represents the head. Self-discipline is the ability to control the inner self of thinking and the outward self of doing. It means exercising good judgment and acting wisely. It means being levelheaded and living that out in practical ways.

Self-discipline is bearing with the temporary discomfort of going to the dentist for the greater gain of healthy and happy teeth. Self-discipline is the discipline of showing up—like that of the pianist who practices every day even when she doesn't feel like it. Not every session may feel inspired, but she's there at the piano when inspiration shows up. Self-discipline helps us keep our core commitments, maintain healthy boundaries, and avoid self-sabotage and destructive behaviors.

In Paul's appeal to Timothy, self-discipline works together with love and power. Without power, we can't get anything done. But power without love and self-discipline can be destructive. Love without power and self-discipline tends to weakness and lack of focus. Self-discipline without power is impossible, and without love, self-discipline is cold and unfeeling. The three need to work together in ministry and in all of life.

So too with our self-care. Self-discipline provides the vital energy that enables us to act in our own best interests, to avoid those things that are bad for us, and to do those things that are good for us but perhaps not the most enjoyable in the moment. Research demonstrates that self-discipline in the form of delayed gratification serves as a marker of successful living. In one long-term study, children who were able to wait well went on to get better grades in school, and forty years later they turned out to be more physically and socially healthy than their peers.[1] Self-discipline contributed positively to their self-care and success.

But the idea of self-discipline as self-care is also limited, for if that's all we had, self-care would be a joyless chore and feel more like self-punishment than anything else. For healthy living, we also need self-care as sheer enjoyment, doing those things that we love, having fun, celebrating life and all of God's goodness, rekindling our hearts and hopes with joy.

---

1. James Clear, "40 Years of Stanford Research Found That People with This One Quality Are More Likely to Succeed," January 23, 2014, https://jamesclear.com/delayed-gratification.

Is it possible to have too much self-discipline in a way that hinders healthy self-care? Does too much self-discipline unnecessarily constrict our lives and squeeze out joy?

What place does joy have in your self-care? Do you do something you enjoy every day? Why or why not?

IS IT POSSIBLE TO HAVE TOO MUCH SELF-DISCIPLINE?

After the death of his wife, Captain Georg von Trapp tried to organize his household with the same precise discipline as his naval command. But his seven lively children kept disrupting his plans, and when their new governess arrived, the captain found himself gradually loosening his tight grip on himself and the rest of the family. As he became less controlling, he also found new love and life.

I don't know how much this story line from *The Sound of Music* reflects the real von Trapp family, but it illustrates how self-discipline is not always truly self-caring. When taken too far, self-discipline can put such a lock on our thoughts and emotions that it shuts out joy and healthy living and strains our relationships.

Yet the letter to the Galatians lists self-discipline as spiritual fruit, which makes it a positive quality. Can anyone have too much spiritual fruit? In this text, however, as in Paul's letter to Timothy, self-discipline doesn't appear alone; instead, self-discipline comes alongside "love, joy, peace, patience, kindness, generosity, faithfulness, gentleness" (Galatians 5:22-23). In this context, self-discipline is not simply a matter of sheer *will*-power and *won't*-power but a gift of God. It's part of a larger picture of well-rounded spiritual growth and maturity alongside other qualities.

To be whole and holy, self-discipline requires patience, kindness, generosity, gentleness, and other qualities to shape it and bring it to maturity. On its own, self-discipline can make us lopsided just like Captain von Trapp, with too much self-discipline and not enough kindness, too much self-discipline and not enough patience, generosity, and gentleness. Instead, we need to temper our spirit of self-discipline with the full fruit of the Spirit.

In the Victorian era, priest and poet Gerard Manley Hopkins (1844–1889) wrote a series of poems that seem to touch on this. In his "Sonnets of Desolation," the poet struggles with anxiety and depression, pouring out his anguish, as in this example:

> My own heart let me more have pity on; let
> Me live to my sad self hereafter kind,
> Charitable; not live this tormented mind
> With this tormented mind tormenting yet.[2]

Later in the same poem, he writes, "Leave comfort root-room." Given the era—mid- to late 1800s—in which he wrote, I doubt that Hopkins had in mind self-care the way we understand it today. Yet his desire to be kind to himself reflects a self-care concern. We might say that instead of "tormenting" ourselves with endless self-discipline, perhaps some of us need more kindness and patience with ourselves.

---

2. Gerard Manley Hopkins, "My Own Heart Let Me More Have Pity On," in *Poems* (London: Humphrey Milford, 1918).

Perhaps that's one reason for the surge of interest in the Danish culture of *hygge* (pronounced hoo-gah).[3] The word has been variously described as a sense of well-being, coziness, comfort, and security. Some trace it back to N. F. S. Grundtvig (1783–1872), a Danish pastor, politician, and writer whose values of simplicity, belonging, and the pleasures of ordinary living helped shape Danish self-identity and culture. *Hygge* means community with enough for all, casual simplicity, comfort food with friends, a mug of hot chocolate by the fireplace, warm socks, and much more.

As *hygge* has become popularized in North America, critics point to its commercialization. Advertisers have indeed been quick to sell *hygge* as a lifestyle of candles, cushions, and other products. But in its most basic form, *hygge* is not a commodity to purchase but a sense of home and welcome relief. For those experiencing the stress and distress of life, *hygge* offers some comfort amid the often uncomfortable circumstances of our world.

Sometimes we need that, don't we? Just as healthy self-care needs self-discipline, there's a place for self-comfort—all in moderation, of course, which is another *hygge* quality.[4] Instead of unbridled consumption, *hygge* is tempered by simplicity, a sense of fairness, and the needs of others. So self-comfort *hygge* style might mean eating a single chocolate chip cookie and not the whole batch, taking time for a little retail therapy

3. Louisa Thomsen Brits, *The Book of Hygge: The Danish Art of Contentment, Comfort, and Connection* (New York: Plume, 2017).
4. Anna Altman, "The Year of Hygge, the Danish Obsession with Getting Cozy," *New Yorker*, December 16, 2016, https://www.newyorker.com/culture/culture-desk/the-year-of-hygge-the-danish-obsession-with-getting-cozy.

without going on a shopping spree you can't afford, and practicing contentment rather than overindulgence.

What would it mean for you to be kind to yourself?
What gives you a deep-down comfort?

THE GIFT OF SELF-CARE: DISCERN SELF-DISCIPLINE AND THE FULL FRUIT OF THE SPIRIT

Sometimes I think I might be too good at delayed gratification. For example, the other day I did go to my dentist, but I didn't go to the library afterward as I had promised myself. I exercised self-discipline to do what I needed to do, but I skipped the joy. Perhaps I didn't need to reward myself this time, and besides, I still have the satisfaction of having gone to the dentist. But I find this happens too often—that I delay so much that the gratification part never actually gets fulfilled.

At other times, I think I need more self-discipline: to work out more consistently, to limit my screen time, to get enough sleep. "I can tell from your teeth that you're not up all night writing your book and drinking coffee," said my dental hygienist. But she doesn't know my late-night weakness for lightly salted potato chips and ginger tea.

Take a few moments to reflect on self-discipline and your own soul. Are you sometimes too hard on yourself? Do you need more self-discipline or more kindness? More gentleness? More patience and generosity with yourself?

■ **CONSIDER 2 TIMOTHY 1:6-7** in the light of self-care. What forms of self-care do you actively practice (power)?

What self-care activities do you enjoy (love)? Which ones take more effort for you (self-discipline)?

■ **CONSIDER GALATIANS 5:22-23** in the light of self-care. How do each of the qualities listed contribute to your well-being? How do they moderate and shape your understanding of self-discipline?

■ **IF YOU NEED** more kindness and patience with yourself, give yourself a break. Look at your to-do list and cross something off without doing it. Plan a fun activity instead. Do something you enjoy or that brings you comfort, not as a reward for something else, but for its own sake. Take comfort in Scripture: read Isaiah 40:1-5; Psalm 23; Psalm 121; Matthew 6:25-33; John 14:27; 2 Corinthians 1:3-7.

■ **IF YOU NEED** to grow in self-discipline, pray and practice, practice, practice. It's really the only way to get better at it. Writing down your progress can help give you focus. Making yourself accountable to another person can offer added incentive. (That's why I've already made my next dental appointment even though it's months away!)

■ **EVEN AS YOU PRACTICE** self-discipline, remember to practice kindness, patience, gentleness, and generosity. These qualities are not only for our relationships with others but for ourselves. In the context of self-care, we might even think of them as self-kindness, self-patience, self-gentleness, and self-generosity.

Part III

MIND

9

Minding Your Focus

You are today where your thoughts have brought you; you will
be tomorrow where your thoughts take you.
—JAMES ALLEN

Mind the gap." On my first trip to London, I heard and
saw those words everywhere: from the unseen voice at
subway stations and on every train to station platforms, mugs,
and T-shirts. On a practical level, the "gap" is the space that
occurs between the subway train door and the station platform. Sometimes it's a step across from the train door onto a
curved platform, or a step down or up, since some trains are
built higher than others. One misstep getting on or off a train
and a passenger could easily twist an ankle, get the wheel of a
suitcase stuck, or have some other kind of accident. "Mind the
gap" serves a practical purpose to warn people to think about
where they're stepping.

As Canadians unfamiliar with the British expression, the members of my tour group would have been more likely to say "Watch your step" or "Pay attention." But we quickly adapted, and "mind the gap" became a kind of inside joke for us. "Mind the gap," we would say at the train station, with knowing smiles. "Mind the gap," we would say if one of us left too large a space as we lined up to go into a museum.

On another level, "mind the gap" reminds me to pay attention to the gaps in my own life: the gap between my God-given dreams and my current reality, the gap between where I believe God is leading me and where I am now, the gap between what I'd like to do and what my time and energy allow. And I mind those gaps not by being annoyed, in the North American sense of the word—as in "Yes, I do mind if you step on my foot." Rather, I am learning to mind those gaps in the British sense of the word—as in remembering, paying attention, and being careful.

Minding those gaps between the life I imagine and the life I live each day is part of self-care. It's important so that I'm not constantly stumbling or getting myself stuck, so that I'm not wallowing in discontent or disappointment or forever running on empty to get ahead. It may not be as simple as stepping over the gap at the train station, but our minds can help us bridge those more personal gaps by determining our goals and priorities, and dealing with distractions and other difficulties along the way. Thinking things through can be a wonderful gift of self-care.

SETTING GOALS AND MOVING THE GOAL POSTS

In Scripture, the word *mind* can mean intelligence, thinking, or understanding. When Jesus tells one of the scribes to love

God "with all your heart, and with all your soul, and with all your mind, and with all your strength," the scribe offers back a paraphrase to love God with heart, *understanding*, and strength (see Mark 12:30-33 emphasis added). When the apostle Paul writes about speaking in tongues, he refers to praying and praising with the spirit and also with his mind, engaging in both ecstatic utterance and words that can be understood, that make sense to himself and others. In this way our minds can powerfully express our devotion to God in worship (1 Corinthians 14:6-19). Yet if we become thoughtless or foolish, the apostle also warns that our minds can lead us astray (2 Corinthians 11:3).

One way to focus our minds is to set priorities. Just as deciding on our core commitments is part of the heart of self-care that defines and shapes our lives, so setting specific priorities and goals with our minds helps us to move forward without stumbling or getting stuck. Setting priorities means taking time to think. It means understanding the difference between what's important and what may appear to be urgent but can actually wait. It means engaging our intelligence, will, and emotions to work toward our goals and to live out the priorities we've chosen.

For my two-month study leave to work on this book, I decided that a good goal would be to complete ten chapters before the end of my leave. I already had a solid outline of all sixteen chapters, a finished introduction, one sample chapter, and a lot of notes with some random parts of the book already written. The goal loomed large, but it had also emerged from my prayers, and at the time seemed entirely doable. So with my goal of completing ten chapters, I started my study leave with high hopes and the best of intentions.

As the weeks went by, however, I realized that my big goal of finishing ten chapters was just too big. So I revised my goal down to nine chapters. But as more weeks went by, I realized that wouldn't work either, so I revised my goal down again to eight chapters. At least I'll be half done with my manuscript when my study leave is over, I said to myself. But by the last weekend, as I was still working on chapter 8, I realized I wouldn't meet that goal either. So I decided that although my study leave would officially end on Sunday, with my leading worship and communion, I'd give myself until Tuesday, since that would be my first official day back in the church office. But when Tuesday rolled around, I needed to move the goal posts one more time to the end of the week, and by then I could finally celebrate my goal!

If you tend to be intimidated by goal setting, just relax and read on. If you regularly set goals for yourself, what one goal are you working on?

GOAL SETTING REVISITED

As I look back on those two months, I realize that for me, setting the initial goal had been easy, even though it later proved impossible to meet. The challenge had been that I simply had too many goals, and not all of them could have the same kind of priority. During my study leave I also kept my weekly blogging schedule, went to a weekend of denominational meetings, prepared and led a seminar, and attended a conference for professional development. During that time, two of our church families also experienced the deaths of family members, so I was asked to lead one of the funerals, and I attended the other. All of these were important, and they reflected my core commitments to pastoral ministry and to my writing. But since my writing goal of finishing ten chapters had been rather arbitrary on my part, I realized that while the writing was important, it could also wait in a way that these other priorities could not.

My experience illustrates several basic principles of goal setting in a way that also reflects good self-care:

1. *Make your goal specific and measurable.* For me, this meant completing ten chapters in two months. For one friend dealing with chronic illness, some days just getting up and getting dressed is a big goal. Others might set financial goals, a certain number of books they want to read, or other personal, family, and vocational objectives.

2. *Write it down, share it with someone else, or both, to build in accountability.* I did both by writing down my goal as a personal reminder and telling my family, friends, and church members.

3. *Have a plan.* My book outline provided the plan, but I could have added mini goals for a certain number of hours or written words a day.

4. *Be flexible.* As much as I tried to work according to my plan, I also set it aside as needed in favor of more time-sensitive priorities, like preparing for the funeral.

5. *Reassess as needed.* I revised my ten-chapter goal to nine, then eight, and when that wasn't enough, I moved the deadlines not once, but twice.

For me, this was all part of good self-care. To address the gap between where I was in my writing and where I wanted to be, I set a goal to help me move toward completing my book manuscript. And when that goal proved impossible, instead of feeling like a failure for missing the mark, I revised my goal over time as needed, even if that also meant moving the goal posts. That's not always possible, but it worked well for me this time. While I didn't meet my original goal of finishing ten chapters in the two months, I was certainly further along than I might have been without any goal at all.

What are the gaps between where you believe God is leading you and where you are now? What goals might God be setting before you to help bridge that gap?

SETTING PRIORITIES

When Martha becomes overwhelmed with her many hosting duties, she complains to Jesus that her sister, Mary, has left her with all the work. But instead of taking Martha's side and asking Mary to help, Jesus gently reminds Martha that "only one thing" is necessary (see Luke 10:38-42). When the psalmist encounters enemies who mean to do him harm, he turns to the Lord in confidence and says, "One thing I asked of the Lord, that will I seek after" (Psalm 27:4). In both cases, the simplicity—and necessity—of choosing just one thing has immense appeal. In a world of multiple tasks and multiple distractions, how refreshing to focus on just one thing—for Martha, for the psalmist, and for us today. In a world of many troubles, what a relief to let them all go and seek single-mindedly for the presence of the Lord.

I see that single-mindedness in Jesus as he faced temptation in the wilderness. Each time the devil tempted him—with bread, with the splendors of the world, with taking God's care for granted—Jesus refused him and responded with the words of Scripture. Jesus grounded his ministry in the Word of God, reading from the scroll of the prophet Isaiah:

> The Spirit of the Lord is upon me,
> because he has anointed me
> to bring good news to the poor.
> He has sent me to proclaim release to the captives
> and recovery of sight to the blind,
> to let the oppressed go free,
> to proclaim the year of the Lord's favor. (Luke 4:18-19)

All four gospels show how Jesus followed through on these words in his ministry as he preached good news, gave sight to the blind, performed many miracles of healing, set people free from sin and shame, and proclaimed that God's kingdom had come. His death and resurrection completed the work—the goal—that God had set before him.

Is it possible to follow Jesus in being just as single-minded about our goals and purpose in life? After all, we have family *and* church *and* work or school (or both). Taking care of our own household *and* volunteering in the community. Going grocery shopping *and* taking the kids to the dentist. Connecting with people in real life *and* with family and friends at a distance. Finding time for work *and* exercise *and* rest. Our different goals seem to vie with one another for limited time and limited resources. How then are we to choose which ones have priority and when?

Good counsel on this abounds. Pray as hard as Jesus did, wrestling with the devil in the wilderness, at times getting up early before anyone else, praying long after others have fallen asleep. Go with your gut, with your feelings from the inside out. Use the A, B, C method of prioritizing in which A stands for those goals or tasks that are vital, B for those less vital but still important, and C for the less important. Follow Stephen Covey's four-part schema to sort tasks as (1) important and urgent; (2) important but not urgent; (3) not important but urgent; (4) not important and not urgent.[1] Follow Marie Kondo and ask what sparks joy in you, which helps both to declutter and organize your possessions and to bring your life goals into focus.[2]

My study leave and all the goals and tasks I had planned were all well within my core commitments, and each sparked joy for me. I even looked forward to a weekend of denominational meetings, for it meant reconnecting with people I hadn't seen for some time and seeing the results of a churchwide project that I had worked on.

While I couldn't say that those meetings or any of my projects were urgent, most involved specific dates that made them time sensitive. So preparing my seminar that was scheduled for early November gave it greater priority than finishing my

---

1. Stephen R. Covey, *The Seven Habits of Highly Effective People* (New York: Simon and Schuster, 2001).
2. Marie Kondo, *The Life-Changing Magic of Tidying Up: The Japanese Art of Decluttering and Organizing* (New York: Ten Speed Press, 2014).

ten chapters by my self-imposed deadline at the end of the month. Besides, my manuscript wasn't due to the publisher until February. Other goals carried more relational weight, so meeting with a family to prepare for the funeral of their loved one clearly became an A-level priority. My inner sense about all of this and my prayers confirmed my direction.

How do you prioritize goals and tasks in your own life? Do you know intuitively and immediately from the inside out, or do you use a deliberate system? Is setting priorities a struggle for you?

THE GIFT OF SELF-CARE: MIND YOUR PRIORITIES

In the late 1800s, Italian engineer and economist Vilfredo Pareto observed that 80 percent of the land in Italy was owned by 20 percent of the people, and he went on to discover that this rough distribution held true in other countries that he surveyed. Since then, the Pareto principle—also known as the 80/20 rule—has been applied to many other contexts, including business, sales, time management, goal setting, and more.

According to the Pareto principle, for example, 80 percent of sales are generated by 20 percent of customers, and 80 percent of the value in a to-do list comes from 20 percent of the items. It's not a precise measurement by any means, and specific results may vary. But as a rough guide, it means that in a to-do list with ten items, completing just two will be worth much more than the rest of the list put together.

- **TEST THE PARETO PRINCIPLE** for yourself. List your goals and tasks for the day and ask yourself: Which one or two of these have more value than the rest of the list? Does the Pareto principle hold true for you? Use it as a helpful guideline for deciding among apparently competing tasks.

- **CONSIDER THE GOALS** that God seems to be setting before you. How do these goals reflect your core commitments? If any do not, prayerfully consider whether you need to rethink your core commitments or your goals.

- **TAKE TIME**. If you tend to deal with goals and priorities on the fly and almost without thinking, take a moment to stop, pray, and address your mind to them more deliberately. If you tend to rely on a system like the Pareto principle or prioritizing A, B, and C, take a moment to stop, pray, and consider what your feelings tell you. Joy, anxiety, and other emotions also contribute to discerning our goals and priorities.

- **FOCUSING ON GOALS** and priorities means letting other things go. That might mean dialing back on some of your other to-dos or eliminating them completely; using social media without being distracted by it (see chapter 10); and managing worry and other negative thoughts and emotions that can drain your energy (see chapter 11). I also find that decluttering my physical environment helps me focus: recycling the junk mail instead of letting it pile up, organizing my closets so I can easily find things, giving away unused items so I have room for the things I use. Take stock of where you need to declutter, then make a start.

10

Minding Your Digital World

Technology is a useful servant but a dangerous master.
—CHRISTIAN LOUS LANGE

Last year, police officers spotted a driver wearing head-phones while driving down a busy city street. When they pulled the man over for distracted driving, they discovered that the driver's headphones were plugged into a smartphone that had been tied to his steering wheel with a piece of string. In between the phone and the steering wheel, the driver had also managed to prop up his computer tablet!

I'm amazed at how far this driver went to maintain access to his devices. Even though the fine for distracted driving is several hundred dollars, and even though over one-quarter of fatal traffic accidents involve some form of distracted driving, he was apparently undeterred. Phone and tablet at the ready, headphones in place, he set out for his day, unaware that his bad example would soon be all over the Internet.

The incident vividly illustrates how tied some of us are to the digital world. Somehow the driver of that car felt he couldn't do without his smartphone and tablet even when he was driving and even though he risked getting a ticket (which was duly issued) or causing an accident (which, thankfully, he managed to avoid that time). Some of us check our email, Facebook, Twitter, or other sites first thing in the morning and the last thing before bed, multiple times throughout the day, and even throughout the night. Whole families sit down together for a meal, but instead of engaging with one another, their eyes remain fixed on their own individual screens.

These are just a few examples of what Tony Fadell calls the "unintended consequences" of technology. A former Apple executive who went on to start his own smart technology company, Fadell now recognizes tech addiction and advocates for greater awareness and control over our digital habits. "We need to learn about these unintended consequences," he says, "and figure out ways to mitigate them and to help us learn a new way of integrating these into our lives."[1]

The way we use or misuse technology in the form of social media and other online engagement affects our self-care too. Such technologies can fragment and reduce our attention span, isolate us from people in real life, distort our view of the world, and persuade us that human identity and value depend on the

1. Quoted in Selena Larson with additional reporting by Laurie Segall, "Early iPhone Designer Calls on Apple to Curb Tech Addiction," CNN Tech, January 11, 2018, http://money.cnn.com/2018/01/11/technology/apple-addiction-kids-smartphones-fix/index.html.

number of likes and shares. Digital distraction might make us "stupid, antisocial and unhealthy," yet the dopamine rush from the constant stimulation keeps us coming back for more.[2]

Just as we mind our focus, can we also mind our digital world as part of good self-care? How can we use these technologies wisely without getting used up ourselves?

MY LIFE WITH SOCIAL MEDIA

The first time I joined Facebook, I lasted less than a day. At the repeated urging of a friend who had posted his vacation pictures only on Facebook, I finally signed up, created my personal profile, happily browsed through his photos, and then promptly deleted my account. I would have stayed, but my profile looked so forlorn without a profile picture and just one friend, and I didn't want the bother of making it look more presentable, so I decided just to shut it down. As with so much online, however, my account didn't disappear forever but simply became hidden and ready to be reactivated at any time.

I joined LinkedIn almost two years after receiving my first of many invitations—and yes, those invitation links still worked even after all that time. I started a blog, joined Twitter, began using Google Plus and Pinterest, although not necessarily in that order, since my online engagement started growing exponentially and I didn't keep track of it all. For some, the names of these different social media platforms might not mean much, but for me and for many they form part of our daily engagement, as much a part of our lives as morning coffee or afternoon

---

2. Eric Andrew-Gee, "Your Smartphone Is Making You Stupid, Antisocial and Unhealthy. So Why Can't You Put It Down?," *Globe and Mail*, January 6, 2018, https://www.theglobe andmail.com/technology/your-smartphone-is-making-you-stupid/article37511900/.

tea, going to work, or spending time with family. In many cases, social media is part of our work and part of the way we connect with family and friends throughout the day or at a distance.

These days I'm on my laptop, tablet, and cell phone a lot, for both work and pleasure. I blog once a week and rarely go a day without Facebook and Twitter. I email and text; I redesigned my own website and started writing and publishing my own ebooks. I've connected with many other writers and writing communities online. While I'm not a digital native like those born into this world of technology, in many ways I've made that world my own.

At the same time, there's a lot I've simply decided to ignore: Instagram, Snapchat, Reddit, and whatever the latest and greatest platforms might be. The Internet is just too big for me to be everywhere, and there are too many different options to engage them all. Besides, if social media is indeed making my attention span shorter, I can't afford to keep dividing it up into smaller and smaller pieces.

In what ways do you engage with the digital world—through a smartphone, tablet, desktop, or other device? What forms of social media and related technologies do you deliberately avoid?

NOT ALL THINGS ARE BENEFICIAL

The caption read "If Jesus were on social media," and the cartoon showed a hand holding a smartphone that read "You have 12 followers." The humor worked for me, since

I recognized the follower language from both Facebook and Twitter set alongside the follower language of Scripture.

What might Jesus do with today's technologies? Would he totally unplug and ignore the digital world at our fingertips? Use every device at his disposal to proclaim the message of God's kingdom? Or handle technology and social media in some other way?

While Scripture does not address such questions directly, it certainly has a lot to say about whom we follow and how we are to treat other people, about the values of God's kingdom and how we are to live. For example, the first letter to the Corinthians addresses sexuality and marriage, filing lawsuits, eating food offered to idols, and other practical issues of their day. In the discussion of each, there is a consistent ethic to live faithfully, to consider the needs of others, and to glorify God. This summary would seem to apply both then and now to the challenges faced by the early church and the challenges we face today with various technologies: "'All things are lawful for me,' but not all things are beneficial. 'All things are lawful for me,' but I will not be dominated by anything" (1 Corinthians 6:12).

Instead of being dominated and overwhelmed by our digital world, what if we engaged only in what is beneficial? What if we sought to live faithfully, to consider others, and to glorify God in the way we use our smartphones and other devices?

Being intentional about our use of technology in these ways might at least begin to address some of those unintended consequences. Instead of unrelenting rudeness, there would be respect; instead of bullying, kindness; instead of arrogance, humility; instead of celebrity, glory to God—as in these words to the saints of the early church:

> Be careful then how you live, not as unwise people but as wise, making the most of the time, because the days are evil. So do not be foolish, but understand what the will of the Lord is. Do not get drunk with wine, for that is debauchery; but be filled with the Spirit, as you sing psalms and hymns and spiritual songs among yourselves, singing and making melody to the Lord in your hearts, giving thanks to God the Father at all times and for everything in the name of our Lord Jesus Christ. (Ephesians 5:15-20)

So also do we need to live wisely and make the most of the time we have. Instead of foolishly going our own way, we can seek to understand and follow the will of the Lord. Instead of getting drunk with wine or excessive online activity or anything else, we can be filled with the Spirit in worship and giving thanks to God.

For me, this means that as much as I love social media and enjoy experimenting with new technologies, I also watch my digital health. To limit my time online, I don't play games. I minimize interruptions by not having email or social media apps on my phone. I try to practice a once-a-week social media sabbath (see chapter 6). My first tweet of the day highlights Scripture to set a positive tone and to remind myself of God's sovereignty over all, including my Internet use. I use a free service to schedule social media so I can manage my posts at times that suit me instead of letting it consume me day and night. I tend to stay out of political or theological arguments, not because I don't have an opinion or don't care, but because the volume and vitriol often seem to outweigh any benefit.

I find these social media strategies essential for my self-care. Without them, the multiple demands of the always-on digital world would overwhelm me entirely. There's always another item in my newsfeed, always another message, always another ad, always another link to follow. Checking just one thing can quickly lead to chasing down one rabbit hole after another until a whole afternoon is gone. Instead of getting lost in that wilderness, I find that the best self-care means choosing how to engage and when.

What do you find beneficial in your digital world, and why?
How do you engage in it to benefit and bless others?

CAN SOCIAL MEDIA MAKE YOU UNHAPPY?

Besides the sheer volume and pace of social media, another unintended consequence is its impact on mental health. According to a recent study, spending time on Facebook makes people unhappy.[3] When everyone else on Facebook and Twitter seems to be having a wonderful time, our own lives can seem rather drab in comparison. Some report trouble concentrating or struggling with FOMO (fear of missing out), while others may feel bad about wasting their time scrolling through content that doesn't satisfy.

When I use social media to compare myself with others, it can make me unhappy too. Someone else always looks happier

---

3. Amy Morin, "Science Explains How Facebook Makes You Sad," *What Mentally Strong People Don't Do* (blog), *Psychology Today*, March 7, 2016, https://www.psychologytoday.com/blog/what-mentally-strong-people-dont-do/201603/science-explains-how-facebook-makes-you-sad.

and healthier, surrounded by their beautiful family, having just published a bestseller and singlehandedly hosted twenty-two people for the most fabulous gourmet dinner the day after returning home from an equally fabulous vacation in Maui. "Comparisons are odious," wrote Christopher Marlowe, and when social media leads to comparing and competing with others, it's no wonder it makes people unhappy.

That's one reason I try to take a social media sabbath each week. That deliberate break disrupts my daily habit and helps to moderate the addictive tendencies. It puts a limit on that constant urge to see what's going on, and reminds me not to get caught up in the endless loop of comparing myself with others and feeling bad when I don't measure up.

Yet when I use social media well, I find that it can also contribute positively to my mental health and well-being. While virtual community can't replace face-to-face community in real life, it has given me a new avenue for making and maintaining friendships, connecting with others who share common interests, and finding and receiving mutual encouragement and support. For me, it's the social part of social media and communicating with others that makes me happy. While I choose not to play games, for others that's also a way of being social or taking a mental health break from other stressors.

People shut in with chronic health conditions can use their devices to access resources, engage a network of support, and connect to the world. Friends dealing with cancer have shared their journey through blogs and other communication networks that allow them to update the people in their lives without having to repeat themselves over and over again.

Social media allows us to widen our circle of prayer beyond our local setting to across the country and around the world.

In what ways has the digital world hindered your mental health and self-care? In what ways has it made a positive contribution?

THE GIFT OF SELF-CARE: BE DELIBERATE ABOUT YOUR DIGITAL WORLD

As Tony Fadell points out, we monitor our weight with a scales, but we tend not to pay the same kind of attention to our use of technology.[4] But why not begin by monitoring your practice? Take a day and count the number of times you check your smartphone, the number of hours you spend looking at a screen, the number of times you text instead of talk in real life. Then reflect on how much of that is beneficial and healthy. If you need to reduce, how will you do that, and when?

Instead of focusing only on avoiding technology, I find it helpful to focus on the healthy alternatives I want to build into my life. Going for a walk outside instead of always working out to a DVD at home. Eating dinner around the table instead of sitting in front of the television. Here are some other ideas you may find helpful.

■ **CHOOSE TECHNOLOGIES** that are right for you. One woman chooses not to use email in favor of the telephone and writing real letters to send by regular post. My husband won't own a smartphone, but he has an iPod so he

---

4. Larson, "Early iPhone Designer."

can listen to sports podcasts while he waters the garden or does other chores.

- **DECLUTTER** whatever devices you have. Delete unused icons, apps, links, and bookmarks to streamline and simplify your use.

- **CONSIDER A ONCE-A-WEEK** social media or technology sabbath. Or unplug every day for an hour. There's an app for that, of course, but you can also do it simply by turning all your devices to airplane mode or just ignoring them for a time.

- **CONSIDER LIMITING** your social media to certain times of the day, perhaps half an hour in the morning and half an hour in early evening.

- **ESTABLISH A FAMILY PRACTICE.** According to author Andy Crouch, when teenagers were asked what they would most like to change in their relationship with their parents, they responded, "I wish my parents were not on their screens and would have paid attention to me."[5] So for your own self-care and for the sake of being present with your children, handle technology with care. One family insists on no mobile devices at the supper table, and that applies equally to parents, children, and any other relatives or guests. Others establish the practice of no screens in the bedroom, and take regular technology breaks.

---

5. Eleanor Barkhorn interview with Andy Crouch, "The Case for a Screen-free Childhood," *Vox*, April 17, 2017, https://www.vox.com/conversations/2017/4/17/15293898/technology-children-boundaries.

11

Minding Your Mental Health

Therefore I tell you, do not worry about your life, what you will eat or what you will drink, or about your body, what you will wear. Is not life more than food, and the body more than clothing?

—MATTHEW 6:25

In this rhetorical question from Jesus' Sermon on the Mount, he prompts his listeners to agree with him. Of *course* life is more than food and the body is more than clothing. We know that. But instead of easing our anxious thoughts, doesn't his question—and our response—just give us more reason to worry?

At least it seems that way to me. For as soon as we have enough food to eat, we start adding to our worries—about the nutritional value of our food, possible *E. coli* contamination, the use of pesticides and other toxic chemicals, child labor and other unjust practices, the high cost of transportation, the impact of preservatives and genetic modification. As soon as we have enough clothes to protect us from the elements, our wants and worries expand, for now we must also be color coordinated, must not wear the same outfit two days in a row, and must be at least minimally fashionable while avoiding sweatshop labor.

We worry about our physical, mental, emotional, and spiritual health, about the safety and well-being of our family, our friends, our reputation, our work, our finances, climate change, war, peace, the state of the church, and the state of the world. Yes, life *is* more than food and the body more than clothing, and our worries seem to multiply accordingly.

Yet to his followers long ago and to our overanxious age, Jesus says, "Do not worry." He appeals to nature, to the birds and flowers, who live apparently free from worry. The birds receive their food and the flowers bloom beautifully. He appeals to reason, which tells us worry is useless in accomplishing whatever it is we worry about. We may worry about our life and health, but worry can't add even an hour to our lives—and may well shorten them, from what today's medical research suggests. Instead of worrying, we are to trust God who provides for us. Instead of worrying, we are to seek after God's kingdom.

If we could only follow these words of Jesus, we wouldn't have to worry about worry as part of self-care! Yet for many of us, worry might seem more complicated than it would have

been for Jesus and his first followers. How are we to understand his counsel to look at how God cares for the birds when
we know about the extinction of whole species of birds? We
might say that humanity's *lack* of worry, or at least appropriate concern, for creation over the years has created even more
for us to worry about.

Two out of five adults in the United States say they worry
every day.[1] In Canada, worry has been called an epidemic.[2]
Beyond that, anxiety disorders are the most common form of
mental illness, affecting an estimated 18.1 percent of the population in the United States, and 12 percent in Canada.[3] Anxiety
disorders include general anxiety, social anxiety, obsessive-
compulsive disorder, and other anxiety-related illnesses.

BUT IS WORRY ALWAYS BAD?

To a certain extent, worry is a God-given normal response
to stress. Worry tells us to pay attention to what's going on
around us, signals a need to adapt in some way, and can
motivate us toward positive change. On a macro level, worry
about climate change has led to increased efforts in research
and more environmentally friendly practices. On a micro level,
a student anxious about final exams might choose to spend
the evening studying instead of going out to a movie. Anxious

1. Roni Caryn Rabin, "Worried? You're Not Alone," *Well* (blog), *New York Times*, May 9,
2016, https://well.blogs.nytimes.com/2016/05/09/worried-youre-not-alone/.
2. Anne Kingston, "The New Worry Epidemic," *Macleans*, February 5, 2014, http://www
.macleans.ca/society/the-new-worry-epidemic/.
3. "Facts and Statistics," Anxiety and Depression Association of America, August 2017,
https://adaa.org/about-adaa/press-room/facts-statistics; "Mental Health and Mental Illness,"
Anxiety Disorders Association of Canada, June 2003, http://anxietycanada.ca/english/pdf/
kirby.pdf.

thoughts and feelings can help identify those things in our world and in our lives that need to change.

In a recent overview of the literature on worry and anxiety, researchers concluded that "although extreme levels of worry are associated with depressed mood, poor physical health, and even mental illness, worry has an upside. We focus on two empirically supported benefits of worry: its motivational benefits and its benefit as an emotional buffer."[4] Their findings confirm the positive role that worry can play in motivating us to identify the need for change, set appropriate goals, and take action. A second benefit is that worry can help prepare us for bad news. It acts as an emotional buffer of sorts: if we receive bad news, we're not quite as devastated, and if we receive good news, we're even more relieved.

But what about the kind of worry that puts us into overdrive and keeps us up all night? The kind of anxiety that blocks out everything else and prevents us from being present to ourselves, to others, and to God? If we understand *worry* and *anxiety* as interchangeable terms, then a certain amount can be healthy and productive. Problems arise only when our worry-anxiety becomes so great that it interferes with our ability to function. The challenge then becomes one of quantity—of how much worry-anxiety we carry.

But instead of simply equating worry and anxiety, author Amy Simpson points out a qualitative difference. She distinguishes between anxiety, which she defines as an initial signal that alerts us to danger, and worry, which she defines as "a

---

4. Kate Sweeny and Michael D. Dooley, "The Surprising Upsides of Worry," *Social and Personality Psychology Compass* 11, no. 4 (April 18, 2017), http://onlinelibrary.wiley.com/doi/10.1111/spc3.12311/full.

choice we make to stay in that place of anxiety that was designed to protect us from immediate danger, not to see us through everyday life."[5] In her view, anxiety would describe the student's initial response to an upcoming exam that motivates the student to study. Living in that anxiety, unable to eat or sleep for days on end, would be worry. Realizing the impact of climate change and engaging it in practical ways might illustrate the functional benefit of some anxiety, while living in a constant state of terror about it expresses worry. In Simpson's words, "Fear and anxiety can be healthy and productive. They can trigger an automatic, lifesaving response. They can motivate us to make wise choices, rescue others and manage risk. Worry, on the other hand, is destructive, unproductive and wasteful."[6]

Do you worry about worry only when it becomes too much? Or do you notice a qualitative difference between constructive anxiety and destructive worry?

THE BLUES AND THE BLAHS

When I wrote about choosing faith over worry, a reader shared this response:

> Over the years, I created my own "worry management process." When I find myself caught by worry or anxiety, I pause and notice it and remind myself that anxiety itself is neither good nor bad. I ask myself: What is it trying to tell

5. Amy Simpson, *Anxious: Choosing Faith in a World of Worry* (Downers Grove, IL: Inter-Varsity Press, 2014), 22.
6. Ibid., 24.

me? Am I in danger? Or am I choosing actions that are un-helpful? Is it something I can act to manage? Or something I need to release? This algorithm sounds simple, but short of being in danger, I often run through it multiple times before a final resolution.[7]

I generally think of an "algorithm" as a complicated computer calculation—like the way Google searches and finds different websites, or the way Facebook decides which of the many posts will actually show up in our newsfeeds. But an algorithm is really any process or series of steps to solve a problem. In this case, the algorithm is a series of questions designed to deal with worry.

I used this algorithm just the other day as a helpful addition to my prayers when I found myself worrying about someone on the brink of making an unwise decision. What was my worry trying to tell me? Was I in danger? No, the situation wasn't about me. Was I choosing unhelpful actions? No, I wasn't directly involved. Was it something I could act to manage? No, I offered what counsel I could, but the choice was out of my hands. Did I need to release it? Yes, the problem wasn't mine to carry.

Did I immediately stop my worrying? Well, no, the algorithm doesn't work quite that directly or instantaneously. It's more mind than heart, more about how to think and pray about a worrisome problem than about resolving the feelings around it. But since the way we think affects the way we feel, I did find it helpful. Taking a step back and reflecting on my worry in the presence of God made me realize that I had taken

7. Kathleen Friesen, March 30, 2015, comment on April Yamasaki, "Three Strategies for Choosing Faith Instead of Worry," https://aprilyamasaki.com/2015/03/30/three-strategies-for-choosing-faith-instead-of-worry/.

on something that rightfully belonged to someone else, and I needed to let it go.

I've found my reader's algorithm for worry so helpful that I've made it my own, with a couple of variations. To her series of questions, I've added another: Is my worry a product of my overactive imagination? Some say that an overactive imagination is one of the occupational hazards of being a writer, but it also seems to be characteristic of the chronic worrier. In the old *Perry Mason* television show, the receptionist Gertie could "take a button and sew a vest on it"—in other words, she could take a small observation and make up an entire story around it. So, too, our worries can sometimes be more imagination than substance, and can appear larger in our minds than in real life. In fact, research indicates that 85 percent of the things we worry about actually end with neutral or positive outcomes.[8]

My other variation is to apply this same algorithm to anger—which can also be an expression of anxiety—and to any kind of stress. Is my worry, anger, jealousy, perfectionism, or other stress coming from my imagination? Am I in danger? Am I acting in unhelpful ways to make my situation worse? Is there some helpful action I can take to manage it? Am I trying to hold on to something that I need to release?

For me, this technique of dealing with worry helps me manage what I call "the blues and the blahs" of life. We all have moments or days that can wear us down, when it may be helpful to take a break, eat from our sad food group, go for a walk, do something fun, take a hot bath, or lift our mood in

---

8. Robert L. Leahy, *The Worry Cure: Seven Steps to Stop Worry from Stopping You* (New York: Harmony, 2006), 18.

some other way. Thinking things through is another way to practice good self-care.

Is there another question you would add to this algorithm for dealing with worry, anger, and stress? How do you manage worry?

MENTAL ILLNESS

For some, however, worry, anger, and other distress may be more serious and ongoing. In North America, about one in five adults will experience a mental illness, including an anxiety-related mental illness, in their lifetime.[9] For them, various self-help measures, along with the support of friends and community, play an important role. But self-care may also include counseling, medication, outpatient care, hospital care, other therapies, or some combination of these.

Both the church and our larger society seem more comfortable with physical illness than with mental illness. We seem to speak more freely about heart attacks or cancer than we do about anxiety disorder or schizophrenia. Yet both physical and mental illness are medical conditions, the two are often interrelated, and there's evidence that depression and anxiety disorders relate to physical changes in the brain.[10] For these reasons, some mental health advocates argue that it would be

9. "Fast Facts about Mental Illness" Canadian Mental Health Association, accessed March 27, 2018, https://cmha.ca/about-cmha/fast-facts-about-mental-illness; Victoria Bekiempis, "Nearly 1 in 5 Americans Suffer Mental Illness Each Year," *Newsweek*, February 28, 2014, http://www.newsweek.com/nearly-1-5-americans-suffer-mental-illness-each-year-230608.
10. Seth J. Gillihan, "Using Brain Scans to Diagnose Mental Disorders," *Think, Act, Be* (blog), *Psychology Today*, May 19, 2016, https://www.psychologytoday.com/blog/think-act-be/201605/using-brain-scans-diagnose-mental-disorders.

more accurate and carry less stigma to speak of "brain illness" instead of "mental illness."

Whatever term we might use, mental illness is not a modern invention, but appears in various places in Scripture. King Saul became so tormented in his spirit that his attendants suggested they find someone who could play the harp for him to relieve his agony. The king agreed to their plan, so they arranged for David to come with his harp. Whenever King Saul felt tormented, David would play, and the king would feel relief.

King Nebuchadnezzar of Babylon suddenly became ill and unable to be with other people or to live in his beautiful royal palace. Instead, he lived outdoors, "ate grass like oxen, and his body was bathed with the dew of heaven, until his hair grew as long as eagles' feathers and his nails became like birds' claws" (Daniel 4:33). Seven years later, his sanity was just as suddenly restored, and he returned to rule over his kingdom.

Psalm 22—which has many parallels with Jesus' death on the cross—has also been understood as the cry of someone with severe depression and anxiety.

My God, my God, why have you forsaken me?
    Why are you so far from helping me,
    from the words of my groaning?
O my God, I cry by day, but you do not answer;
    and by night, but find no rest. (Psalm 22:1-2)

Jesus met a disturbed man living out among the tombs who would often howl and cut himself with stones. He had at times been restrained with chains to prevent him from hurting himself and others, but he broke free and wandered through the mountains night and day. Today, his symptoms might be diagnosed as some form of schizophrenia.

Then and now, we live in a fallen and broken world in which physical and mental illness form part of our reality. Worry and anxiety remain part of human life. Whether or not our symptoms arise from mental illness, and however our feelings and responses might vary in quantity or quality, all people are made in the image of God. All are meant to be treated with the same dignity and respect that Jesus extended to the man among the tombs and to everyone he met.

In what ways might history and Scripture help us feel less alone in our worry, or anger, or stress? What other stories from the Bible make you feel less alone when you consider your own strong emotions?

THE GIFT OF SELF-CARE: NURTURE YOUR MENTAL HEALTH

If you or others are concerned about a possible mental illness, please consult your doctor, counselor, or other healthcare professional. Admitting you need help can be difficult, but it is also a positive step of self-care.

For ways we can all nurture our mental health, consider the following.

■ **THINK POSITIVE.** A steady diet of negative people, negative news stories, and negative thoughts can be hard on mental health. Take a break from the negativity, cull your Facebook feed, choose carefully the people you spend time with, and nourish your mental health with art, beauty, and God's magnificent creation. As the apostle Paul wrote from prison: "Finally, beloved, whatever is true, whatever is honorable, whatever is just, whatever is pure, whatever is pleasing, whatever is commendable, if there is any excellence and if there is anything worthy of praise, think about these things" (Philippians 4:8).

■ **KEEP A GRATITUDE JOURNAL** by writing down a few things that you're thankful for each day. If you're feeling ambitious, assign a number to each one, and see how long it takes to get to a hundred or a thousand or more. If you're having a hard day, start with lament. I find that writing out my worries makes them seem smaller. As my lament gives way, I'm able to move on to giving thanks for God's care.

■ **CONSIDER** what practical assistance might help you cope with your worry, anger, or other distress: a night off, someone to keep you company, an entertaining diversion, someone to babysit or drive you to an appointment, a ready-made meal, financial help, prayer, going to church, a support group, community service. Who might be able to help you help yourself?

■ **REALIZE** you are more than your worry, anger, stress, or mental illness. You are God's beloved, God's masterpiece created new in Christ Jesus, fearfully and wonderfully made!

12

Renewing Your Mind

Just the knowledge that a good book is awaiting one at the end of a long day makes that day happier.
—KATHLEEN NORRIS

Sister Mary loved to read. After her graduation from eighth grade, she entered the School Sisters of Notre Dame convent in Baltimore, Maryland. When she made her religious vows five years later, she began teaching middle schoolers while continuing with her own studies. When she finally retired from full-time teaching at the age of seventy-seven, she continued to serve as a teacher's aide into her mid-eighties. In the years that followed, Sister Mary kept reading, remained active in her community, and continued to be keenly aware of the world around her. She appeared a shining example of living and aging with grace until her death at the age of 101.

After her death, researchers discovered that while Sister Mary's mind had remained clear, her brain showed the characteristic signs of Alzheimer's disease. Given the lesions in her brain, they would have expected a significant decrease in brain functioning. Yet her last cognitive tests had been well within the normal range.[1] Somehow, Sister Mary had managed to renew her mind despite the physical changes in her brain.

Was it all her reading that helped Sister Mary? What other factors might have contributed to the renewing of her mind? How might we care for and renew our minds at one hundred years old or at any age?

THE NUN STUDY

Sister Mary's story is just one of the fascinating outcomes of a long-term study of aging and Alzheimer's disease begun by David Snowdon in 1986. Dubbed "the nun study," the work centers on 678 members of the School Sisters of Notre Dame, all over seventy-five years of age, who agreed to participate by sharing their stories and medical records and undergoing various cognitive and other tests. In 2001, the initial findings and practical lessons appeared in the award-winning book *Aging with Grace: What the Nun Study Teaches Us about Leading Longer, Healthier, and More Meaningful Lives,* and the research work has continued since then.[2]

Because the nuns live in community and share a similar lifestyle, many of the usual environmental variables are already

---

1. David A. Snowdon, "Aging and Alzheimer's Disease: Lessons from the Nun Study," *The Gerontologist* 37, no. 2 (1997): 150–56.
2. David A. Snowdon, *Aging with Grace: What the Nun Study Teaches Us about Leading Longer, Healthier, and More Meaningful Lives* (New York: Bantam, 2001).

accounted for. All of the nuns participating in this study share the same gender, race, and marital status, and they have other similarities in terms of type of work, housing, diet, and habits, including not smoking and consuming little or no alcohol. As a relatively homogeneous group, they make an ideal test population, with convent records providing a wealth of information in the form of birth certificates, family histories, medical records, and other data. The nuns who participated even agreed to donate their brains after their deaths.

Snowdon was particularly interested in why some brains lose cognitive functioning with aging while others do not. To this end, he examined the nuns' autobiographies, which they had written and submitted as young women about to take their religious vows. The researcher was looking for both the density of their ideas and their grammatical complexity. He then compared his findings with their cognitive functioning some fifty-eight years after their written statements. His conclusion? In each case, the nuns with low idea density and low grammatical complexity as young women also had low cognitive test scores in their later years. Among those nuns who had died, those with low idea density in their written work earlier in life showed evidence of Alzheimer's disease in their autopsy results, while those with high idea density showed no evidence of the disease, although Sister Mary would later prove to be an exception.[3]

These results suggest a practical application for renewing our minds by working at our reading and writing skills

3. Paul Spector, "Nun Watching: What Sisters Are Teaching Us about Aging," *Huffington Post*, December 6, 2017 https://www.huffingtonpost.com/paul-spector-md/nun-watching-what-sisters_b_12387956.html.

throughout our adult lives. One theory is that learning new things creates new neural pathways, so our brains have greater resiliency. Another posits a threshold model, in which dementia occurs only when our cognitive reserve falls below a certain level, so greater cognitive functioning early in life gives us a greater reserve.

How regularly do you read and write? What other intellectual pursuits do you enjoy? What new things are you learning or would you like to learn?

THE MIND OF CHRIST

At Sister Mary's memorial service, it was said that one day she had asked her doctor whether he had been giving her medicine to prolong her life. Her doctor replied, "Sister, it's not my medicine that's keeping you alive. It's your attitude!"[4]

By all accounts, Sister Mary had indeed been a cheerful presence in her community, interested in other people and world events, with an outgoing personality and a warm laugh. She prayed regularly for the needs of the world, designating one day of the week for each of the continents. Her life had been marked by service throughout her teaching career, and when the nuns received the invitation to participate in the study on aging and Alzheimer's disease, she had been the first to volunteer.

In her life of service, I see in Sister Mary the mind of Christ. Not in the sense of intellectual ability, necessarily, but in the sense of "the mind" as understanding, as an orientation and

---

4. Snowdon, "Aging and Alzheimer's Disease," 150.

attitude toward life. One of the earliest Christian hymns describes it this way:

> Let each of you look not to your own interests, but to the interests of others. Let the same mind be in you that was in Christ Jesus,
>> who, though he was in the form of God,
>>> did not regard equality with God
>>> as something to be exploited,
>> but emptied himself,
>>> taking the form of a slave,
>>> being born in human likeness.
>> And being found in human form,
>>> he humbled himself
>>> and became obedient to the point of death—
>>> even death on a cross. (Philippians 2:4-8)

The earthly life of Christ was marked by humility and service. From the humble circumstances of his birth to his ministry of preaching, teaching, and healing, Jesus put the needs of others before his own need for rest and safety. Even in his so-called triumphal entry into Jerusalem, he entered the city not as a great war hero who would take the city by force but as one who would soon be arrested, tortured, and executed like a criminal.

In many ways, that seems just the opposite of self-care, for Jesus lost his life most cruelly. Yet three days later, God raised him from the dead in a mighty act of vindication. The ancient hymn continues:

> Therefore God also highly exalted him
>> and gave him the name
>> that is above every name,
> so that at the name of Jesus
>> every knee should bend,

in heaven and on earth and under the earth,
and every tongue should confess
    that Jesus Christ is Lord,
    to the glory of God the Father. (Philippians 2:9-11)

Jesus the Christ had risen to new life! The one who had humbled himself has now returned to glory.

If we are to renew our minds in the broader sense of our attitude and outlook on life, we need this bigger vision of the humility and glory of the Lord. We'll need to renew ourselves in humility and service as Jesus did, and as Sister Mary seemed to do. While this might seem counterintuitive as a self-care practice, it's entirely consistent with Jesus' teaching that those who lose their life will find it. As a friend and advocate for homeless people says, "The fact is, we will never be mentally or socially healthy unless we are also serving others."

If serving others is essential to our mental and social health, we might say that serving others is itself a form of self-care. In what ways do you agree with that statement? In what ways might you disagree?

A GROWING EDGE

As I reflect on Sister Mary's example, I'm struck by the powerful combination of renewing her mind both in the intellectual sense and in an attitude of serving others. That same combination surfaced again when I wrote about self-care and invited readers to respond. One reader asked, "Does self-care include steps to avoid 'routinization' or losing an intentional growing edge?" He went on to elaborate:

Once we have finished formal education and training, we have the option of coasting along and sticking to what we already know. But there seems to be so much more waiting to be explored and developed. Intentionality means we are self-starters and creators of our own program of ongoing growth. We have the option of devising a plan for ourselves, each of us, and pursuing it for the sake of service to others; at the same time it serves our self-care needs. Each of us as leaders need to face the question: what is your cutting edge during this time? What are you focusing on? Being intentional and curious is energizing and becomes a source of blessing to our people.[5]

While his comment addresses leaders, I understand the term quite broadly. In whatever leadership capacity we find ourselves—church members, parents, grandparents, employees, employers, students, volunteers in the community—we can continue learning and exploring. We can be intentional, take initiative, and create a program of ongoing growth uniquely tailored to our situation that both serves others and provides for our self-care. While my reader didn't mention the nun study, his comments echo familiar themes of both intellectual engagement and service.

When I was first called into pastoral ministry, I had a graduate education in biblical studies but no formal pastoral training. I had some practical experience as a college instructor and church council member but no professional ministry experience in a church setting. You might say I knew just enough to be dangerous, and enough to know that I had huge gaps in both knowledge and experience. In those early

5. John H. Neufeld, October 9, 2017, comment on April Yamasaki, "How Do You Handle Self-Care?," https://whenyouworkforthechurch.com/2017/09/21/how-do-you-handle-self-care/.

years, I identified my growing edge clearly in pastoral care and practical theology, and most of my reading and professional development centered there. I thought of that mainly in terms of service for the church. Looking back, however, I realize that it was also a form of on-the-job self-care as I grew in effective ministry. I engaged in ongoing learning with the intention of blessing others, but it also blessed me, for it combined service, intellectual growth, and self-care all at once.

As parents of children-suddenly-turned-teenagers, a couple might enroll in a parenting class to help them grow as parents while also serving others by haring what they're learning. They practice self-care as they become more comfortable with setting appropriate boundaries for themselves and learning how to keep them. A grandparent might read the newspaper every day, doing the crossword puzzle to exercise his mind and paying special attention to the sports news so he can relate more closely to his grandson, who is an avid football fan. As we take care to be renewed mentally, we also renew our relationships and serve others.

Where is the growing edge in your own life—in your workplace, or more personally? How might you renew your mind with a combination of intellectual engagement, serving, and self-care?

While I want to be deliberate about learning, serving, and growing, I know that for my mind to be renewed, I also need times of rest. Sometimes I need to not think. I need to stop taking in more words and sharing more words with others. I need to step away from the information overload and the noise around me. I need to remember these words of Jesus: "Come to me, all you that are weary and are carrying heavy burdens, and I will give you rest. Take my yoke upon you, and learn from me; for I am gentle and humble in heart, and you will find rest for your souls. For my yoke is easy, and my burden is light" (Matthew 11:28-30).

So if you already feel worn out by serving, or if learning new things is overwhelming you, then give yourself a pass. Come to Jesus, and set down your burdens. Be gentle with yourself as he is gentle with you. Rest. Let God bear your yoke and burden. Let God renew your mind and spirit.

After his disciples returned from a busy time of teaching among the villages, Jesus encouraged them to rest awhile. While Jesus gave himself fully to God's work, he also took time to rest. In fact, while his disciples worked hard to get their boat across the sea, Jesus was fast asleep.

As the book of Hebrews instructs, our chief end is not work but rest, promised by God long ago to people wandering in the wilderness and searching for home, and that promise holds for us today as well: "So then, a sabbath rest still remains for the people of God; for those who enter God's rest also cease from their labors as God did from his" (Hebrews 4:9-10).

So don't feel guilty if you need to rest. That is God's work of renewal for your mind and body. We can rest in our sacred pauses, rest on the Sabbath, rest our minds, rest from serving, and rest with a good night's sleep. All are foretastes of that eternal rest.

THE GIFT OF SELF-CARE: LEARN, SERVE, REST

Our minds find renewal as we learn, serve, and rest. At times, these three may overlap; at times they may feel quite separate and may address a distinctly different need. Here are a few ideas for each, to mix and match or to spark your own ideas.

- **LEARN:** Read the newspaper. Browse the new books in the library and choose one. Listen to an audiobook. Subscribe to a podcast. Build something. Try a new recipe. Go to a lecture. Take a course, whether for credit or audit. Write your autobiography, as the young nuns did. Choose a subject and devote a couple of hours a week to study. Learn a language. Teach Sunday school. Ask questions. Be curious.

- **SERVE:** Share a hobby or skill. Read to someone who can't. Volunteer at a local food bank. Sing on a music team. Give someone a ride. Hold the door open for the person behind you. Bake muffins to give away. Offer to help a neighbor. Stop to give directions to a stranger who's not sure which way to go. Pray—you could try Sister Mary's way of praying around the world, with a day for each continent. Mail a greeting or get-well card.

- **REST:** Spend an evening at home. Sit and daydream. Go for a walk and don't take your earbuds. Read a book for sheer enjoyment. If you normally read nonfiction, pick up a novel or read a book of poetry. Watch television or take in a movie. Laugh. Spend time with your kids, and let them decide what you'll do together. Play a game. Do Sudoku or a crossword, jigsaw, or other puzzle. Go out to eat, or bring food in. Play volleyball or some other sport you enjoy.

Part IV

STRENGTH

13

Strength in Weakness

Take care of your body. It's the only place you have to live.
—JIM ROHN

Practically speaking, motivational speaker Jim Rohn makes a good point: take care of your body, because "it's the only place you have to live." It's the only body you have. As human beings, we are both body and soul, both outwardly physical and inwardly spiritual, both what we can visibly see and touch and what we invisibly know and feel. To be alive at all means to have a living body, so self-care applies to heart, soul, mind, and body. We turn now to our bodies, represented by the word *strength*.

In Scripture, the word *strength*, in the broadest sense, means the ability to do something, to have the power and capacity to make something happen. It takes physical strength to walk, and it takes the strength of will and motivation too. It takes strength to speak and find community with other people, strength to build a house and turn it into a home, strength to do anything. The Old Testament preacher says, "Whatever your hand finds to do, do with your might" (Ecclesiastes 9:10). That means, put everything you've got into whatever you do. Do it with your strength. Do it with passion!

Like heart, soul, and mind, strength has multiple meanings, and it shares some of the qualities associated with the other three gifts. When the apostle Paul says, "Be strong in the Lord and in the strength of his power" so that you may withstand temptation (Ephesians 6:10-11), that strength includes our whole capacity to do the right thing—physically, mentally, spiritually, with all our heart and soul. When the apostle Peter writes, "Whoever serves must do so with the strength that God supplies" (1 Peter 4:11), that includes the strength of mind to plan and make decisions, the strength of body to follow through with action, the strength of heart and soul to serve gladly and with humility. Once again, the four gifts of heart, soul, mind, and strength work together as one.

YOUR BODY, GOD'S TEMPLE

In addition to the sheer physicality of human life, the apostle Paul, writing to the Corinthian church, offers a theological reason for tending to our bodies—take care of your body, because it's the temple of the Holy Spirit: "Do you not know that your body is a temple of the Holy Spirit within you, which you have from God, and that you are not your own? For you were bought with a price; therefore glorify God in your body" (1 Corinthians 6:19-20). To be sure, Paul did not have self-care on his mind as he wrote these words. His letter focused rather on sexuality, marriage, prostitution, lawsuits, food sacrificed to idols, and other matters of concern to the Corinthian church. But his basic principle applies to life in the body whatever the specific issue might be: we do not belong to ourselves but to God, for the human body is a temple of the Holy Spirit.

Earlier in the same letter, Paul describes the church as a temple—not the church building as we might think of it today, but the church as the people of God. If the people were a building, they weren't any old building, but a temple—a sacred space, made beautiful as a work of art, meant for worship and communion with God, for gathering together and thinking big thoughts. So when Paul says your body is a temple of the Holy Spirit, he speaks of the physical body as sacred, a work of art and worship, set apart for God.

We are to use and care for our bodies as God's temple for worship and service, to pray and care for others, to give glory to God. What we do in and through our bodies matters, because we belong to God. That makes caring for our bodies an act of stewardship, as author and speaker Parker Palmer points out: "Self-care is never a selfish act—it is simply good stewardship of the only gift I have, the gift I was put on earth to offer others. Anytime we can listen to true self and give the care it requires, we do it not only for ourselves but for the many others whose lives we touch."[1]

---

1. Parker J. Palmer, *Let Your Life Speak: Listening for the Voice of Vocation* (San Francisco: Jossey-Bass, 2000), 30–31.

If our bodies are sacred, then caring for our bodies is holy work. How might that change your attitude toward caring for your body?

STAYING STRONG

I never cared much for sports and staying strong. "You're a hothouse flower," my mother would say, and yes, this hothouse flower would rather stay cozy at home with a good book than go ice skating. I enjoyed gabbing with friends on the sidelines instead of joining the game. When everyone in my class had to play softball, I would generally stand out in right field, alternately terrified that the ball would come my way and daydreaming about something else entirely. I succeeded in intramural basketball only because I hung back and played my position, staying out of the scrum of the other girls pouncing on the ball.

Yet I kept active almost despite myself because my two feet served as my main form of transportation. Back and forth to elementary school and high school, twice a day, since I most often went home for lunch. Two miles to the hospital where I served as a youth volunteer, and two miles home again. In university I walked with friends every morning at least a mile from the farthest—and cheapest—student parking lot to a building on the other side of campus . . . and back again, another mile, at the end of the day.

Today when it comes to sports, I'm still more of a spectator than a team player. But walking doesn't fit into my day as naturally as it used to, so I need to be more deliberate about exercising. Some days I wear a pedometer to make sure I get my ten thousand steps a day. I set aside time for walking or doing step aerobics, lifting weights, or doing some other kind of workout. I'd still rather be reading a good book, but I've also learned the value of staying strong with regular exercise. Besides, I feel better when I work out regularly.

A mother of teenagers says her self-care means increasing exercise. "It seems biblical, after all," she says, "since Jesus walked a lot." In the ancient world, the most common form of transportation was walking, so yes, Jesus and every able-bodied person in his day would have walked a lot. Physical activity was a way of life—sowing seed, gathering the harvest, grinding wheat, baking bread, carrying water, washing clothes, and other daily tasks kept people so active that they didn't need to count their steps or plan for aerobic activity or lift weights.

In our more sedentary culture, in both Canada and the United States, guidelines for physical health recommend 150 minutes of moderate to vigorous activity each week for all adults, plus muscle and bone strengthening activity at least two days a week.[2] That means I can walk just thirty minutes a day for five days each week and lift weights the other two days. Or, since the guidelines count activity in periods of ten minutes or more, the walking could be twice every day for ten minutes each time, with an extra session thrown in at some point during the week. Overall, the guidelines seem quite moderate to me, flexible up or down in intensity and duration according to ability, available time, and personal preference.

2. See Canadian Society for Exercise Physiology, "Links to CSEP Guidelines," accessed March 30, 2018, http://www.csep.ca/guidelines; Office of Disease Prevention and Health Promotion, "Physical Activity Guidelines: Adults," accessed March 30, 2018, https://health .gov/paguidelines/guidelines/adults.aspx.

Yet just one in five adults in Canada and one in three adults in the United States meet these guidelines, and I often struggle to meet them too.[3] I'm too busy. I'm getting a sore throat. I'll just skip today and do a bit more tomorrow. But tomorrow often brings the same litany of excuses, and soon a whole week or more has gone by. When that happens, I have to go back to walking instead of step aerobics, and I have to use lighter weights than usual until I build up my fitness again.

How does your physical activity compare to the recommended guidelines? What might be a reasonable fitness goal for you? Be aware that any guidelines may vary for specific individuals depending on age, health, and physical ability.

ACKNOWLEDGING WEAKNESS

Although I'm definitely not an athlete, I love the athletic metaphors in Scripture that express the strength of the human body. Believers "run with perseverance the race that is set before us," and the apostle Paul describes himself and others as running or racing, and as pressing on toward the finish line. We are to train our bodies like boxers and be self-disciplined (see Hebrews 12:1; Philippians 3:12-14; 1 Corinthians 9:26-27).

---

3. Public Health Agency of Canada, *Health Status of Canadians 2016* (Ottawa, 2016), 33, https://www.canada.ca/content/dam/hc-sc/healthy-canadians/migration/publications/ department-ministere/state-public-health-status-2016-etat-sante-publique-statut/alt/pdf-eng .pdf; U.S. Department of Health and Human Services, *Facts and Statistics*, President's Council on Sports, Fitness and Nutrition, accessed April 15, 2018, https://www.hhs.gov/fitness/ resource-center/facts-and-statistics/index.html.

Yet Scripture also acknowledges human weakness. The Gospels speak of many who were sick or lame, suffering and dying. Even those who were healed by Jesus—and those he raised from the dead—did not live forever. Then and now, human life on earth is short and fragile, like grass that soon withers or "a mist that appears for a little while and then vanishes" (see Isaiah 40:6-8; James 4:14). Jesus himself grew hungry, thirsty, and weary. Even as he referred to his body as God's temple, in the same breath he spoke of its destruction, by which he meant his death. Three days later, God would miraculously raise him to new life, but in his earthly body Jesus also experienced weakness, vulnerability, and death.

As much as we might want to stay strong, we humans are frail creatures, limited by weakness, disease, disability, and mortality. As theologian J. I. Packer writes,

> When the world tells us, as it does, that everyone has a right to a life that is easy, comfortable, and relatively pain-free, a life that enables us to discover, display, and deploy all the strengths that are latent within us, the world twists the truth right out of shape. That was not the quality of life to which Christ's calling led him, nor was it Paul's calling, nor is it what we are called to in the twenty-first century. For all Christians, the likelihood is rather that as our discipleship continues, God will make us increasingly weakness-conscious and pain-aware.[4]

The apostle Paul certainly experienced that in his life. In a second letter to the Corinthians, he writes of his many trials—afflicted and persecuted, beaten, shipwrecked, and subject to many other hardships and dangers. If all that weren't already too much, he had a persistent "thorn" in his

---

4. J. I. Packer, *Weakness Is the Way: Life with Christ Our Strength* (Wheaton, IL: Crossway, 2013), 53.

flesh that would not go away despite his persistent prayers. It may have been chronic migraines or some other physical pain, perhaps depression or some other condition. But instead of removing it, God answered Paul's prayer with this: "My grace is sufficient for you, for power is made perfect in weakness" (2 Corinthians 12:9).

I can imagine Paul's initial disappointment—frustration even, for he had prayed for release over and over again. "How long, O Lord?" he might have prayed with the psalmist (Psalm 13:1; 35:17; 79:5; 89:46). I sometimes lament this in my own prayers. Yet eventually he made peace with God's answer and with his personal situation, for he wrote to the Corinthians: "So, I will boast all the more gladly of my weaknesses, so that the power of Christ may dwell in me. Therefore I am content with weaknesses, insults, hardships, persecutions, and calamities for the sake of Christ; for whenever I am weak, then I am strong" (2 Corinthians 12:9-10).

In his weakness, Paul found a new kind of strength given to him by the grace of God. This was not a physical strength that rid him of his pain or ailment, but a strength of spirit that overcame all his hardships and physical weakness—a strength that had him rejoicing in the Lord.

While in prison, Paul would make a similar point: "I can do all things through him who strengthens me" (Philippians 4:13). He was not saying that he could set himself free from prison, or become a wealthy man, or do whatever he wanted. Instead, his comment focused on being content whatever his circumstances—whether wealthy or poor, well fed or hungry, physically strong or needy, he could rely on God's strength in any situation.

A note I received from a church member with chronic health problems exhibits this same strength in weakness. "Because my body is the temple of the Holy Spirit I am still to glorify God with it, in all its aches, pain, and dysfunction," she wrote. Whatever our strengths and weaknesses, to God be the glory! Whatever our age and stage of life, even for those whose bodies are frail, who must deal with disease, disability, and their own mortality, to God be the glory!

How do you experience strength and weakness in your body? Have you also experienced strength in weakness, and if so, how?

THE GIFT OF SELF-CARE: BUILD UP STRENGTH, BE GENTLE WITH WEAKNESS

"I have now reached the point in life where, inevitably, I am wearing out physically," says J. I. Packer in his mid-eighties. "God doesn't allow us to stay with the idea that we are strong. We may have that idea, but the Lord is going to disabuse us one way or another, and it will be good for us and it'll give glory to him."[5]

Given both the strength and frailty of our physical selves, caring for our bodies would seem to require two movements: both building up the strength we have, and being gentle enough to prevent injury, both striving for the goal, on the one hand,

5. "J. I. Packer, *Weakness Is the Way*" video, April 18, 2013, produced by Crossway, 2:57, https://www.youtube.com/watch?v=seBsfKi-v2w

and resting, on the other. When I first started working out with weights, I learned that my muscles needed both training days and rest days. Working out every day might lead to fatigue and even injury from overuse, so recovery days were essential.

Depending on our age, health, and current level of fitness, our need for movement and rest will vary. For some dealing with acute or chronic illness, lifting a teacup or even swallowing may be too much. For some who are strong and healthy, the eight-pound weights I use would be laughably light. So I offer the following forms of caring for your body only as examples. Please be aware that they may or may not be appropriate for you depending on your situation.

- **BREATHE**. Close your eyes. Smile. Take a long, hot shower. Have a warm bath. Try dry skin brushing. Nourish your skin with body lotion. Get a massage, a manicure, or a pedicure. Wear something that feels good against your skin.

- **STRETCH**. Raise your arms above your head; sit in a chair and straighten your legs one at a time; stand up and touch your toes. Sit cross-legged. Explore the gentle movements of qigong, which can be done standing, sitting, or even lying down.

- **MOVE**. Walk around the block. Take the stairs instead of the elevator. Vacuum, wash the floors, or do other household chores that keep you on the go. Wrestle with your kids. Try yoga, tai chi, or other low-impact exercise.

- **WORK UP A SWEAT**. Bike. Jump rope. Play tennis. Dance your heart out. Run. Do interval training. Enter a fun run or road race to add interest and challenge yourself. Take a spin class.

■ **REST.** Curl up with your pet. Sit in the sun for fifteen minutes (and don't forget the sunscreen). Nap. Get out in the garden and touch the earth. Give yourself permission to be still and do nothing.

14

Strength in Healthy Sleep Habits

Now I lay me down to sleep, I pray the Lord my soul to keep.
—EIGHTEENTH-CENTURY BEDTIME PRAYER

On my best nights, I'm in bed somewhere between ten thirty and midnight, sleep solidly until morning, and wake up before the seven fifteen alarm that I set just in case. One night, however, still fueled by an afternoon coffee that I don't usually drink, I stayed up until three in the morning. I didn't feel at all tired, so I did some writing, paid some bills, made granola, cleaned up the kitchen, read the newspaper, finished the crossword puzzle and Sudoku, until I finally decided I should go to bed.

The next day, I mentioned my late night (early morning, actually) to a friend. "This is why I'm not a coffee drinker,"

I said. "I get so wired by caffeine that even one cup in the middle of the afternoon keeps me up half the night because I'm just not tired."

My friend looked back at me strangely. "You mean you didn't feel tired at all?" she asked slowly, with a trace of wonder in her voice. "I don't even know what not being tired would feel like."

SLEEP DEPRIVATION AS A WAY OF LIFE

I don't even know what not being tired would feel like. My friend is not alone in her bewilderment. According to an international study by the insurance company Aviva, Canada and the United States are tied as the third most sleep-deprived countries in the world. Out of thirteen countries surveyed, the United Kingdom tops the list, with 37 percent of people reporting a lack of sleep, followed by Ireland with 33 percent, and the United States and Canada both at 31 percent.[1] Studies within Canada and the United States report similar results. An analysis by the Centers for Disease Control and Prevention indicates that, on average, 35.2 percent of Americans need more sleep.[2] The Canadian Men's Health Foundation found that one-third of Canadian men ages thirty to forty-nine get less than seven to eight hours of sleep a night, and nearly half report waking up feeling tired.[3]

1. Rebecca Joseph, "Canada Third Most Sleep-Deprived Country: Study," Global News, October 29, 2016, https://globalnews.ca/news/3033503/canada-third-most-sleep-deprived-country-study/.

2. "Short Sleep Duration among US Adults," Centers for Disease Control and Prevention, last modified May 2, 2017, https://www.cdc.gov/sleep/data_statistics.html.

3. Dr. Larry Goldenberg, "Study Finds a Third of Canadian Men Are Sleep Deprived," Canadian Men's Health Foundation, July 25, 2016, https://menshealthfoundation.ca/study-finds-third-canadian-men-sleep-deprived.

While I didn't feel tired at three in the morning or even at seven when I woke up without my alarm after just four hours of sleep, by most objective standards I was still sleep deprived. Four hours is definitely less than the seven to eight hours of sleep recommended by most health professionals. In fact, sleep scientists consider four hours to be our "core" sleep requirement, which is just enough for the body to function at the cellular level. Five to seven hours is "luxury" sleep, which allows for proper brain functioning; seven to eight hours is "optimal" sleep for peak performance; while anything over nine hours may be oversleeping.

To my mind at least, this explains why I apparently functioned just fine on four hours of sleep that day—because I had at least achieved my core sleep, and it was just one night. But I couldn't do that night after night and still expect to feel alert day after day. In my case, a late afternoon coffee had resulted in an artificially induced wakefulness. Other culprits that can disturb sleep include family and work stress, being too hot or too cold, eating too close to bedtime, not getting enough exercise, napping during the day, too much screen time, too much light from our devices even when we're not using them, and being overworked, overtired, and just too busy. Like Elijah running for his life from Queen Jezebel until he finally fell asleep exhausted under a tree, many of us are running through life too, falling asleep exhausted and waking up tired—and with much less reason than Elijah.

Besides measuring hours of sleep per night, sleep researchers also assess sleep efficiency, which is the number of hours slept divided by the total number of hours in bed. If a person sleeps six hours but keeps waking up and tossing and turning throughout the night for a total of two hours, the sleep efficiency is six hours out of eight hours, or 75 percent. Sleep scientists say that's bordering on insomnia, while 85 percent sleep efficiency is considered normal, 90 percent and up very good, and 100 percent a likely indicator of not enough time in bed to get adequate sleep. My own experience testifies to that, for when I stayed up until three in the morning, my sleep efficiency came close to 100 percent—I slept solidly for almost all four of the hours I spent in bed, but it simply wasn't enough.

How many hours of sleep do you typically get in a night? Calculate your sleep efficiency ratio by dividing the number of hours you sleep by the total number of hours in bed. Do you generally wake up feeling rested, or still tired?

SLEEP AS SELF-CARE

If our lack of sleep were only about feeling tired, we might simply dismiss it as a minor discomfort and carry on. But as I'm learning, sleep deprivation can affect our physical, mental, emotional, and spiritual health in ways that we may not realize. While the occasional restless night might seem relatively harmless, a chronic lack of sleep can lead to low energy and fatigue, diminished concentration and attention span, increased irritability and anxiety, poor judgment, impaired motor skills, and serious accidents, like falling asleep at the wheel while driving. Poor sleep can also suppress the immune system and contribute to heart problems, diabetes, and digestive problems. Poor sleep can even make us gain weight.

While a good night's sleep is not exactly a cure-all, the benefits are clear. Cognitive functioning, memory, and mood all improve. The body becomes more equipped to cope with stress and physical health challenges. "Sometimes the most spiritual thing you can do is get a good night's rest," I heard one pastor say at a retreat. We might also say that sometimes the best overall self-care is getting a good night's sleep.

Scripture speaks positively of a good night's sleep as a reward for a good day's work and as a sign of trust in God (Ecclesiastes 5:12; Proverbs 3:21-26). "I will both lie down and sleep in peace; for you alone, O Lord, make me lie down in safety," writes the psalmist (Psalm 4:8).

Yet too much sleep could also be a sign of laziness (Proverbs 6:6-11). In an ancient agrarian culture that depended on sunrise and sunset without the benefit of electricity, missing the daylight hours to sleep meant missing valuable time for work.

Wealth does not guarantee a good night's sleep, for eating too much can disturb sleep (Ecclesiastes 5:12). King Hezekiah could not sleep because of an unnamed illness that brought him to the point of death and distressed him bitterly (Isaiah 38:1-16). When King Ahasuerus could not sleep, he set his mind to work, had his servants read to him from the book of records, and decided to reward Mordecai for foiling an assassination attempt against him (Esther 6:1). There's no way of knowing whether the weight of the king's responsibilities contributed to his sleeplessness, but at least he managed to put his sleepless hours to good use.

Other parts of Scripture portray sleeplessness in a positive light. When King Darius is manipulated into consigning Daniel to death in the lions' den, he spends a sleepless night fasting for God's deliverance, and in the morning rejoices to find that Daniel has indeed been spared. In this case, the king's sleeplessness demonstrated his agony over being forced to condemn Daniel against his will, and was rewarded by God's miraculous intervention (Daniel 6:1-23). Centuries later, the apostle Paul lists sleepless nights as part of the proof of his faithfulness and a sign of God's commendation of his ministry (2 Corinthians 6:5; 11:27).

So is sleep a blessing, a sign of laziness, or evidence of abiding trust in God? Does sleeplessness indicate unhealthy stress, anxiety, and overwork, or can it also be an expression of integrity and deep commitment to faithful service? Instead of setting out a standard formula, the witness of Scripture seems to vary according to the context and particular situation. Perhaps the psalmist best expresses the interplay between sleep as a conscious act of self-care and sleep as a gift from God.

> Unless the Lord builds the house,
>   those who build it labor in vain.
> Unless the Lord guards the city,
>   the guard keeps watch in vain.
> It is in vain that you rise up early
>   and go late to rest,
> eating the bread of anxious toil;
>   for he gives sleep to his beloved. (Psalm 127:1-2)

How often do you experience sleeplessness, and under what circumstances? If you can't sleep at night, do you generally get up and try to be productive, or do you simply rest?

THE SCIENCE OF SLEEP

My husband says that I have a special gift for sleeping through the night until I wake up rested and ready for my day. He usually wakes up too early and still tired after a restless night of waking up several times. That's made both of us curious about what sleep researchers call good "sleep hygiene": the practices and conditions that contribute to a good night's sleep. We've experimented with many of these, like limiting caffeine in the late afternoon and evening, ending screen time at least thirty minutes before bed, going to sleep at the same time each night, and waking up at the same time each morning. While some of these have been helpful, others have made little difference. Except for my reaction to caffeine, I tend to sleep well even when I break all the rules.

Our various sleep experiments made me even more curious when I saw an article about the perfect night's sleep "according to science."[4] In a recent study from the United Kingdom, the best sleep hygiene apparently includes:

- Painting your bedroom white
- Maintaining a room temperature of 16 degrees Celsius (60 degrees Fahrenheit)

4. Krista Thurrott, "How to Get a Perfect Night's Sleep According to Science," Yahoo Style Canada, September 29, 2017, https://www.yahoo.com/news/get-perfect-nights-sleep-according-science-160521580.html

- Going to bed at 10:39 p.m.
- Using two pillows
- Lying on your right side
- Turning off your phone thirty-seven minutes before trying to sleep[5]

The precise numbers reported in the study made me smile. I wondered, would the time difference between the United Kingdom and the west coast of Canada, where we live, make a difference to that 10:39 p.m. bedtime? How much difference would it make to end screen time at thirty-seven minutes instead of half an hour before trying to sleep? Maybe it was our skepticism, but even though we tried to get the perfect sleep according to the science of this particular study, it didn't seem to make much difference. We soon fell back into our usual habits.

Our experience mirrors the experience of most people, for despite the latest science and despite the most well-known sleep hygiene practices, most people tend to fall back on their own personal preferences. Some of that may be out of habit and the ever-present pull of technology. Says Jas Bagniewski, the founder of the company that commissioned the sleep study, "We have some way to go towards actually putting this knowledge into practise: whilst we all know that looking at our phones isn't helpful for example, almost a third of us are still doing it less than 10 minutes before trying to drop off."[6]

What's more, for many people today, personal experience trumps any kind of science. "I only need four hours of sleep

5. George Harrison, "Survey Reveals the Secrets to a Good Night's Sleep," *The Sun*, September 26, 2017, https://www.thesun.co.uk/fabulous/4550812/secrets-good-nights-sleep/.
6. Quoted in ibid.

a night," insists one high-energy friend, even though he recognizes that's just half the recommended amount. "As I've grown older, I need less sleep," says another, even though our need for sleep does not decrease with age but in fact remains constant throughout our adult years.[7]

Yet whatever our individual and subjective preferences might be, we all need sleep. Whether you need to go to bed exactly at 10:39 p.m. or to get exactly eight hours of sleep may well vary from person to person. But good self-care means being self-aware. Do you have trouble getting to sleep at night? Do you wake up multiple times and have trouble falling back to sleep? Are you so tired in the morning that you can't keep your eyes open? While anyone might have difficulty sleeping on occasion, chronic insomnia or other sleep disturbances may signal a need for medical attention. When in doubt, or if you have questions, consult your doctor or other medical practitioner.

*What are your best self-care practices
and conditions for getting a good night's sleep?*

THE GIFT OF SELF-CARE: PRACTICE GOOD SLEEP HYGIENE

There's a wealth of advice on good sleep habits, and the consensus seems to include going to bed and getting up at the same time, eating regular meals and taking any medications

7. "Aging and Sleep," National Sleep Foundation, accessed March 22, 2018, https://sleep foundation.org/sleep-topics/aging-and-sleep.

at the same time of day, avoiding caffeine, getting exercise (as long as it's not too close to bedtime), and avoiding screen time at least half an hour before bed.

Of course, knowing these things and putting them into practice are not the same. So if your knowledge exceeds your practice at this point, choose one or more of these consensus practices to try. You may also want to consider some of the following helpful, but perhaps less well-known, practices.

- **DRINK MORE WATER.** While some advise restricting water intake during the evening and before bed, being properly hydrated can actually help with sleep. I always thought I drank enough water until I discovered that the Mayo Clinic recommends a daily intake of ten eight-ounce glasses for women and thirteen eight-ounce glasses for men! Of course, that average will vary according to weight and activity, but I imagine it's still a lot more water than I might normally drink without thinking about it.

- **IF YOU CAN'T SLEEP,** at least get some rest. If you wake up repeatedly throughout the night or too early, instead of getting up while you're still tired, stay in bed if you can, with your eyes closed. You might even drift off to sleep without realizing it.

- **TAKE A SHORT NAP** in the late morning or early afternoon. A long nap late in the afternoon can leave you feeling groggy and interfere with sleeping at night, but a quick ten- to twenty-minute nap earlier in the day can be refreshing and can banish that mid-afternoon slump.

■ **ESTABLISH A RITUAL.** Just as children benefit from a nighttime routine that helps them get ready for bed, as adults we can also benefit from a routine that helps us relax and fall asleep. Try a bath and a hot cup of herbal tea. Read Scripture and pray. Or take ten minutes for some light reading, journaling, or coloring. I usually write down the top two or three things I need to do the next day. While even thinking about tomorrow might be too stimulating for some, I find that simply listing a few priorities helps me to relax, commit them to God, and put them out of my mind. I can sleep knowing that God is at work and those things will keep until morning.

15

Strength in Healthy Food Choices

It is more fun to talk with someone who doesn't use long, difficult words but rather short, easy words like "What about lunch?"
—A. A. MILNE, *WINNIE-THE-POOH*

My desk at home is right next to the kitchen, so as I write I'm often cooking or baking, or sometimes all three at the same time. One day I might make a batch of cranberry coconut muffins, followed by a pan of homemade granola. Or vegetarian chili topped with corn bread, tofu and cabbage with black bean sauce, or baked salmon with a thin spread of Dijon mustard and fresh dill clipped from the garden. Not all at once, of course, and not every day, but you get the idea—I like to cook and bake almost as much as or more than I like to write.

Today I have beef bourguignon simmering on the stove—part celebration, since I finished another chapter of the book yesterday; part thrift, since the bottle of wine came to us as a gift; part experiment, since I've actually never made this classic French dish before. It seems the ultimate comfort food—bubbling happily away in the background and filling the house with warmth and a fruity, mouth-watering aroma. But is it a healthy choice? I wonder. After all, it's mainly beef and wine with just a few carrots and mushrooms. I might need to add a salad. And eat vegetarian tomorrow.

Knowing what to cook can sometimes be a challenge. I eat mainly dairy free. My husband eats soy free. We both avoid nitrates. Other family members avoid gluten. A friend is allergic to corn and always carries an epinephrine autoinjector in case of a bad reaction. Others have experimented with the hundred-mile diet, the Whole30, and other diet plans that promise participants will lose weight, feel more energetic, prevent disease, and eat more responsibly for the planet and for the sake of all living creatures.

Can we do all that for our own self-care and for the sake of others? In the bewildering array of different dietary needs and diets, with different health and allergy requirements, given different personal preferences and various food choices, how do we care for our bodies and physical strength by making healthy food choices?

SHOULD WE ALL BE VEGETARIANS?

When King Nebuchadnezzar laid siege to Jerusalem and took over the land of Judah, he took the healthiest and most intelligent young men captive for his own service (Daniel 1:1-21). He provided them with daily rations of food and wine and arranged for their education in the language and culture of the Babylonians so that at the end of three years they would be able to serve in his palace. But Daniel and his three colleagues—Hananiah, Mishael, and Azariah—refused to accept the king's food and drink.

At first reading, this refusal might seem strange, for the four men apparently cooperated with the king's plan for their training and service. When the palace master replaced their Israelite names with new names derived from Babylonian deities, they seemed to accept that as well: Daniel (which means "God is my judge") became Belteshazzar (a reference to the Babylonian god Baal), Hananiah (which means "God is gracious") became Shadrach (a reference to the Babylonian god Aku), Mishael (which means "who is like God") became Meshach (another reference to the Babylonian god Aku), and Azariah ("God has helped") became Abednego (a reference to the Babylonian god Nebo). Their new names, cultural environment, and education may well have been deliberate attempts to weaken their identity with the God of Israel; accepting the king's food and drink would have taken them even further in that direction.

By refusing the king's rations, Daniel and his colleagues remained free to follow the dietary restrictions of the religious law, and they could be sure that none of the food they ate would have been used in the idol worship of the Babylonians. What's more, in the ancient world, food and drink often served as a sign of covenant, and while Daniel and his colleagues were willing to serve the king in his court, their covenant loyalty belonged to their God alone. Accepting the king's food and drink would have sent the wrong message, so Daniel asked for only vegetables to eat and water to drink.

At first the palace master was afraid that the young men would become weak on their vegan diet. But when they appeared healthier than ever at the end of their ten-day trial, he agreed to continue. They remained faithful to God, and God blessed them with both good health and success in their service to the king: "To these four young men God gave knowledge and skill in every aspect of literature and wisdom. . . . In every matter of wisdom and understanding concerning which the king inquired of them, he found them ten times better than all the magicians and enchanters in his whole kingdom" (Daniel 1:17, 20).

On the basis of Scripture, one might argue in favor of a vegan diet, for in creation, God says, "I have given every green plant for food" (Genesis 1:30), and certainly Daniel, Hananiah, Mishael, and Azariah seemed to thrive on their diet of vegetables and water. Today we know that a plant-based diet of whole grains, fruits, and vegetables means less stress on the planet and less saturated fat in our bodies, which can also lower the risks of heart disease and obesity. Canada's Food Guide—originally developed in the 1940s to address nutrition and wartime rations—is now being revised with more emphasis on vegetables, fruits, and plant-based protein.[1] In the United States, dietary guidelines also encourage a variety

---

1. Health Canada, "Summary of Guiding Principles and Recommendations," last modified April 4, 2017, https://www.foodguideconsultation.ca/guiding-principles-summary. The new guide is expected to be released in stages, beginning in 2018.

of vegetables, fruits, and whole grains while limiting saturated and trans fats and added sugar.[2]

At the same time, both guides include dairy and meat as healthy sources of protein, calcium, and other nutrients that may not be as readily available in a vegan diet. In the ancient world, Jewish dietary laws included certain meats with specific instructions on how to prepare them, and the priests ate a portion of the animal sacrifices. Jesus attended weddings and other celebrations where meat would often be part of the feast, and in his story of the return of the prodigal son, the father tells his servants to prepare a fatted calf for the celebratory meal.

So yes, I enjoyed cooking my beef bourguignon, and I am happy to report that it looked as beautiful and tasted as delectable as it smelled. We ate with a prayer of thanks and great delight! But for us it's not a dish to eat every day, even with heart-healthy whole grain bread and a green salad. Tomorrow I'm looking forward to my tofu and bok choy.

What's in your lunch today? Do you make a conscious effort to eat less meat? Why or why not? How many servings of fruits and vegetables do you normally have in a day?

THE HOW OF EATING

Daniel and his colleagues refused the king's rations as part of their larger concern to live faithfully toward God even while in captivity. Their land overtaken, pressed into the king's service,

---

2. Office of Disease Prevention and Health Promotion, "Top 10 Things You Need to Know about the 2015–2020 Dietary Guidelines for Americans," January 7, 2016, https://health.gov/news/dietary-guidelines-digital-press-kit/2016/01/top-10-things-you-need-to-know/.

and assigned Babylonian names, they remained loyal to God's covenant by keeping the food laws. In time, Hananiah, Mishael, and Azariah would refuse to worship the Babylonian gods and be condemned to death by fire. Daniel would continue to pray to God three times a day, and be cast into a den of lions. But God would save all four of them, and in the meantime, they remained faithful (see Daniel 3, 6).

When the Corinthian church faced a controversy over food, it was again part of a larger issue of faith. Was it permitted to eat food that might have been offered to an idol? On the one hand, the apostle Paul does not forbid it, for idols are not real gods and there is only one God and one Lord, Jesus Christ. But not everyone understands that, and if eating food offered to idols would wound the faith of others, he argues that it is wiser to refrain (1 Corinthians 8:1-13). He makes a similar point in his letter to the Romans: "Everything is indeed clean, but it is wrong for you to make others fall by what you eat; it is good not to eat meat or drink wine or do anything that makes your brother or sister stumble" (Romans 14:20-21).

In each of these examples, the focus is actually less on what to eat or not to eat, and more on *how* to eat. For Daniel and his colleagues, the how meant eating in faithfulness to God according to the covenant. For the apostle Paul and the early church, the how meant eating with consideration for brothers and sisters in the Christian community. This same concern about how to eat is reflected also in the discussion of the Lord's Supper: eat in a spirit of unity, in remembrance of the Lord's death, not rushing ahead to eat your fill while another goes hungry (1 Corinthians 11:17-34).

Whatever our particular needs and diet issues, the how of eating contributes to our self-care. Giving thanks before a meal reminds us that our food is an expression of God's love and care for us. Slowing down to eat and savoring the taste of our food can add to our enjoyment and aid digestion. Eating in a spirit of unity and sharing food is not only for the Lord's Supper, but a principle of good eating every day that both cares for ourselves and considers others.

Food and faith often appear together in the Gospels. Jesus prayed before feeding the crowds. After his resurrection, two of his disciples recognized him only when they broke bread together. How does the combination of food and faith contribute to the way you care for your body?

EAT WITH JOY

In her book on joyful eating, Rachel Marie Stone begins with examples of conflicted eating and related issues, including eating disorders, obesity and weight loss, industrial agriculture, poverty and starvation, and unjust labor practices. Then, drawing on biblical perspectives and her own journey with food, she concludes:

> Eating with joy means accepting food as God's gift. . . . It means choosing food, as far as we are able, that affirms a flourishing life for the land, for the animals and for the people that bring us our food. It means eating food with others in ways that lead to our mutual health and flourishing. And it means embracing our creativity as people made in the

image of the Creator God to prepare food in ways that celebrate God's gift while bringing enjoyment to all our senses.[3]

In this, Stone echoes the words of the ancient preacher: "Go, eat your bread with enjoyment, and drink your wine with a merry heart" (Ecclesiastes 9:7). The book of Proverbs also speaks of eating with joy where love is, in contrast to eating with trouble and hatred.

All the days of the poor are hard,
    but a cheerful heart has a continual feast.
Better is a little with the fear of the Lord
    than great treasure and trouble with it.
Better is a dinner of vegetables where love is
    than a fatted ox and hatred with it. (Proverbs 15:15-17)

This glad eating is clearly meant to be shared with others in the household and extends also to those in need, for "those who are generous are blessed, for they share their bread with the poor" (Proverbs 22:9).

Today as we care for our bodies by making healthy food choices, we also need this vision that acknowledges food as a gift from God, that includes creativity and caring for others, that is life-giving for ourselves and for all creation. It's not only about *what* we eat but *how* we eat, for ourselves and for the sake of others.

How would you describe your attitude toward eating?
Is it conflicted, joyful, or something else?

---

3. Rachel Marie Stone, *Eat with Joy: Redeeming God's Gift of Food* (Downers Grove, IL: InterVarsity Press, 2013), 159.

THE GIFT OF SELF-CARE: CONSIDER WHAT AND HOW YOU EAT

Since bodily health and dietary needs vary so much from person to person, it doesn't make sense to offer specific food recommendations here. For some, dairy may be a healthy part of a daily diet. Since too much dairy can make me walking-into-walls tired and give me a migraine, it's not a good self-care choice for me. "No longer drink only water, but take a little wine for the sake of your stomach and your frequent ailments," wrote the apostle Paul to Timothy as a young church leader (1 Timothy 5:23). While that may have been a helpful folklore remedy for Timothy, it wouldn't do for anyone with a sensitivity to alcohol or struggling with addiction.

So if you have questions about what to eat, it's best to consult your doctor, nutritionist, or other health professional who can assist you in addressing your particular health needs. The food and fasting ideas below may or may not be suitable for you, and are offered here only as examples.

- **FOR BETTER DIGESTION** and greater enjoyment of your food, slow down to eat. Use all your senses to savor the sight, the smell, the textures, the taste, even the sound of whatever you're eating. Cook or bake something that smells delicious. Feast your eyes on a table set with fresh flowers and real napkins. Use the good dishes. Take a moment of silence or offer a prayer before you eat.

- **IF YOU'D LIKE** to increase the amount of vegetables and fruits in your diet, consider finishing your meal with salad or fruit instead of a sweet dessert, or limiting meat to one meal a day, or planning a once-a-week Meatless Monday.

- **FAST.** In university I would sometimes do a juice fast for spiritual and health reasons. Now my fasting is more modest and more partial, but I still think of it as part of my self-care. Like giving up potato chips for Lent. Or fasting from snacking in between meals, and drinking more water instead.

- **TREAT YOURSELF** to takeout. When I'm feeling pressed for time and have a counter full of dirty dishes at home, this is one of my favorite self-care food choices. It eliminates or cuts down on cleanup so I have time to tackle that backlog of dishes, and it can be healthy too. Think fresh salad rolls from the Vietnamese restaurant, a healthy wrap from the sandwich shop, or roast chicken from the deli with your own stir-fried vegetables and rice.

- **IF YOU OFTEN EAT ALONE,** plan time to eat with others. "When people eat alone, they tend to overeat or eat too little, to eat food that is of poorer quality and to enjoy it less," writes Stone.[4] So take care of yourself and share your table with family, friends, and others.

---

4. Ibid., 75.

16

Strengthening Your Self-Care

The Lord is the everlasting God, the Creator of the ends of the earth. He does not faint or grow weary; his understanding is unsearchable. He gives power to the faint, and strengthens the powerless.

—ISAIAH 40:28-29

When I'm at church on a Sunday morning, I'm usually up in front welcoming everyone to worship, leading prayer, or preaching. But one Sunday morning, as our youth led worship, I sat in the balcony with my husband. "How does it feel to have a week off?" one of our church members asked me.

"Just great," I said with a smile. "And our youth did an amazing job leading us this morning."

Later, I wondered about the conversation. Did he really think I had a week off just because I wasn't up front? I was pretty sure he had been joking, but I felt a bit uneasy. Our exchange made me think: What is it that I actually do during the week? And does anyone but me and the Creator notice?

For example, that week I led our staff team meeting; had separate conversations with different staff members; met with our Vietnamese ministry support team; prayed through our church prayer list; made a number of phone calls; talked with several members who stopped by the church; prepared for a wedding that Saturday; did some advance work on my next sermon; and sent forty-one emails related to worship planning, personnel, the start of the Sunday school year, and other ministry matters. And that's just what I did Tuesday, Wednesday, and Thursday. My days were full. But when I read a list of ministry to-dos written by another pastor, I noticed something missing from my list: self-care.

Wait a minute. You mean self-care is actually part of my job too?

SELF-CARE AS A WAY OF LIFE

I had always thought of self-care as something I did on my own time. Like doing the *New York Times* crossword every morning, trying to eat healthy, getting my ten thousand steps each day, or writing in my journal. While I might take a nap on a Sunday afternoon and call it self-care, I wouldn't dream of doing that on a Tuesday and counting it as church time! I have always thought of self-care as part of my life, not part of my job.

Yet in the face of increasing challenges in the workplace, some are arguing for self-care in and at work. According to clinical psychologist Dana Gionta,

> Many of us associate self-care with getting adequate exercise and proper nutrition. Self-care practices are often done either before or after work, but not during. Being at work, however, does not negate the need for continued self-care. Considering the total number of hours we spend weekly at work, it is actually more important to our well-being and for our relationships, to practice good professional self-care while at work.[1]

By "good professional self-care" Gionta doesn't mean taking that afternoon nap, or idly scrolling through Facebook for an hour, or playing a video game and calling it self-care. Instead, she lists:

- Creating a healthy work space for yourself
- Developing a short list of priorities for each day
- Minimizing procrastination
- Taking intermittent breaks, like a lunch break or talking with coworkers
- Setting and maintaining professional boundaries

I had never thought of these as self-care, but Gionta's perspective gave me new insight. In my mind, planning my day had always been squarely in the work category as part of my job. But now I realized that it was part of my self-care too. For while setting appropriate priorities made my work more effective, it also reduced stress and so contributed to my overall well-being both on and off the job. Minimizing procrastination

---

1. Dana Gionta, "7 Steps to Better Employee Self-Care in the Workplace," *Occupational Hazards* (blog), *Psychology Today*, November 10, 2008, https://www.psychologytoday.com/blog/occupational-hazards/200811/7-steps-better-employee-self-care-in-the-workplace.

helped me get things done, and using my energies more wisely at work meant more energy overall.

Talking with people in a variety of occupations confirmed my new understanding. "Of course, self-care is part of the job," said one nursing supervisor. "Taking regular breaks is essential, especially on long shifts." For a construction worker, wearing the right safety gear is both part of the job and part of good self-care. For an office worker, the right chair can make for better concentration on the job and personal relief from chronic back pain. For businesspeople and others regularly assigned cell phones, tablets, or other devices, setting boundaries around communication manages expectations on the job and keeps work from taking up all their family and personal time too.

So self-care isn't only about "my" time. It's not only about what I do in some separate compartment of my life. That's why the stories and examples I've shared in this book come from my life and the lives of others, from church and home and school and work and everywhere—because self-care belongs to every sphere of life. At its best, self-care *is* a way of life, a gift that sustains each of us as we serve God and serve other people. My new appreciation for self-care as a way of life gradually developed into this book as I became eager to share what I've been learning.

Think of your own occupation or the occupation of someone you encounter in your daily life—a student, a homemaker, a car mechanic, a store clerk, the mail carrier. How is self-care part of the job?

SELF-CARE FOR EVERYONE

Just as self-care embraces all of life, every stage of life seems to generate questions of self-care. "Do you ever worry?" asked the children's storyteller one Sunday morning. Even the kids in kindergarten nodded their heads. "Worry is like being scared," said one of the older children. "But worry doesn't help,"' said another.

"For us, self-care means not being 'on' all of the time," says one ministry couple. "It often involves turning off our caring, and having family time on our own. Otherwise, we carry things so deeply, and it weighs us down."

A young adult says, "Between work and school, I'm feeling overwhelmed and can't take on any more commitments."

An older adult also comments on the busyness of life: "One thing I see in myself and other seniors is the tendency to keep so busy and never take time to 'Be still, and know that I am God.' In part it's a continuation of finding our identity in what we do, a socially acceptable way of hanging on and denying our mortality."

"I am almost eighty years old," says an elder. "I hope that you will include people my age in self-care too."

Consider your own stage of life and the questions of self-care that you face. How have these changed over time for you? What new self-care challenges might you expect in the next five years?

GROUNDED IN GOD'S CARE

When I first shared my plans for this book, an author friend responded, "Writing to deadline will require a lot of self-care, so you'll be living what you write." Honestly, I'm still working on that, just like everyone else, still doing what I can with on-and-off success, falling off the wagon and getting on again. I certainly haven't arrived at any ideal place of self-care, and I suppose I never will. As the circumstances of my life keep changing, my self-care needs and practices will keep changing too.

None of us knows what self-care challenge might be just around the corner. Yet whatever comes our way, our self-care can remain grounded in God's care for us. As the prophet says, "In returning and rest you shall be saved; in quietness and in trust shall be your strength" (Isaiah 30:15). In the original context of this verse, Isaiah's people had placed their trust in their own judgment and in the strength and speed of their horses. But the prophet urges them instead to rely on God. Ultimately for us as well, when our strength fails, when we feel powerless, we can rely on God who strengthens us.

> Even youths will faint and be weary,
>   and the young will fall exhausted;
> but those who wait for the Lord shall renew their strength,
>   they shall mount up with wings like eagles,
> they shall run and not be weary,
>   they shall walk and not faint. (Isaiah 40:30-31)

These are powerful, prophetic words that look forward to that day when all God's promises will be fulfilled. On that day, sorrow and sighing will be no more, we will find rest for our souls, and heaven and earth will be made new (Isaiah 35:10; 51:11; Matthew 11:29; Revelation 21:1). A "glorious inheritance" awaits us as we look forward in hope and wait for the Lord (Ephesians 1:18).

But do these words also apply to our lives today? Can we make sense of them in a world that groans even now under the weight of suffering, oppression, and injustice? Where is God's strength for those weak from hunger? Where is renewal for those crying for relief from suffering? For this world, the prophet's insistence on trusting God might seem rather naïve—part ancient myth and part misguided sense of first-world privilege. But I see it rather as a radical claim in a world where God's care is sorely needed, and where Jesus' great commandment calls us with even greater urgency to love God and love our neighbor as ourselves.

A woman desperately trying to care for herself and her two children appealed to Elisha for help. Her husband had been a prophet like Elisha, but he had died, and she had been forced into debt to feed her family. Now the creditor threatened to take her children as slaves in payment. She had nothing else to give but a single jar of oil. So Elisha told the woman to borrow vessels from all her neighbors, return home, shut the door, and start pouring her bit of oil into the empty vessels (II Kings 4:1-7).

God created a miracle that day as the woman kept pouring oil. The oil did not give out until she had filled all the empty vessels to the brim. When she was finished, she had enough oil to sell to pay her debt and support herself and her children. In her need, she had asked Elisha and all her neighbors for help, and God worked through their sharing in a mighty way. Without all her neighbors to supply the vessels, the oil may not have been enough to meet her need. Without God's abundant mercy, she would have lost her children.

In the face of desperate need in our world today, God still chooses to work through neighbors—through you and me and all of us. Like the woman's neighbors, we too have something to offer in the face of deep need, even if it's only an empty vessel waiting to be filled by God. And like the woman, we too can act in faith, trusting that God's abundant mercy will not fail. Her self-care and ours is grounded in and animated by God's care.

What would it look like for you to care for yourself and others out of God's strength instead of relying solely on your own strength? To serve out of God's abundance instead of scarcity?

THE GIFT OF SELF-CARE: PRACTICE SUSTAINABLE SELF-CARE

As I continue seeking self-care, I'm grateful for God's four gifts of heart, soul, mind, and strength. I've also come to realize that these four gifts open us up to many more gifts, many more creative ways to experience self-care grounded in God's never-ending care for us. From honoring our core commitments to getting enough sleep, from feeding our souls to developing our minds—self-care embraces all of life at every stage.

At the same time, these gifts are not simply once and done, close the book and move on to something else. The gifts of self-care work most effectively and grow stronger when they're used again and again, when they become a regular practice. So strengthen your self-care by making it sustainable.

■ **MAKE SELF-CARE** a regular practice. Some love the repetition and beauty of established rituals, such as always lighting a candle to begin Sabbath rest or always reading for half an hour before going to sleep. Consider adding a ritual of self-care to your daily routine, or if you prefer a freestyle approach, choose a different practice each day. One morning I might light a candle as I journal, another morning I might skip the candle but have a cup of my favorite tea. One day I might skip my journal, candle, and tea altogether and take a sacred pause with *lectio divina* later in the day. While self-care can be the same thing every day, it doesn't have to be. But with some form of regular practice, self-care can become a way of life.

- **REALIZE** that your self-care needs change over time. If a ritual has become ho-hum and too matter of course, consider whether God is calling you to stay with it and deepen your practice or to make a change. If you used to walk to work as part of your self-care but now have switched jobs and that's no longer possible, consider adding some other form of self-care. Parents with teenagers may have different self-care needs and opportunities now that their children are older. Recently retired persons will have different self-care needs and opportunities than when they were employed.

- **DITCH THE GUILT.** Give yourself permission to take care of yourself. You are God's work of art and precious child, with a special commission to love God and love others as yourself. Enlist the support of family and friends. Start a self-care support group for prayer and mutual encouragement.

■ **WHEN EVEN SELF-CARE** seems like too much, give yourself permission to rest. When even prayer seems too difficult, know that God's Spirit "intercedes with sighs too deep for words" (Romans 8:26). Lean on Jesus. Allow God's strength to sustain you.

Acknowledgments

Writing this book has been a gift to me, and I have many people to thank.

- To all my readers past, present, and future: You inspire and challenge me, and I pray this book will speak into your life as you have spoken into mine. Thank you for sharing your stories, your thoughtful questions, and words of encouragement.
- To everyone at Emmanuel Mennonite Church: You've made me a better pastor and writer. Your support has been key in seeing this book to completion. I am deeply grateful for the regular study leaves and days off devoted to this project, and even more for your trust that has grounded me and set me free to write.
- To the Redbud Writers Guild and my online community of writers and readers: You're the reason I love social

media. Finding kindred spirits who cheer each other on has turned my virtual world into real community. Thank you for the warmth of your welcome, connection, kindness, and support.

- To Amy Simpson for her glad yes to write the foreword: Thank you for sharing some of your own journey with self-care. Your books are wise and wonderful, and I'm grateful for your words of grace.

- To all those at Herald Press: You make a great team! Thank you especially to Amy Gingerich, who read one of my blog posts on self-care and enthusiastically responded, "This should be in a book!" I am grateful as well for Valerie Weaver-Zercher, who shepherded me through the various stages toward publication, and to Reuben Graham for the book design that so beautifully expresses heart, soul, mind, and strength.

- To all my family and friends, especially to those who may be surprised to see themselves in this book: When drawing on published sources, I've included appropriate notes for reference, but when borrowing from the lives of those around me, I've omitted names for the sake of privacy. Thank you for your understanding and patience, and for being part of my life and this book.

AND NOW, THANKS BE TO GOD, for all your presence, goodness, and care:

> The Lord is my strength and my shield;
> in him my heart trusts;
> so I am helped, and my heart exults,
> and with my song I give thanks to him. (Psalm 28:7)